WAR WILL NOT TAKE PLACE

J.R. FREARS
JEAN-LUC PARODI

WAR WILL NOT TAKE PLACE

The French Parliamentary Elections
March 1978

1979

C. HURST & COMPANY · LONDON

First published in the United Kingdom by
C. Hurst & Co. (Publishers) Ltd.,
1-2 Henrietta Street, London WC2B 8PS

ISBN   0-905838-20-3

A *nos pères*

    RUSSELL FREARS

et

    ALEXANDRE PARODI

Printed in Great Britain

ACKNOWLEDGEMENTS

The authors wish to express their gratitude to the Nuffield Foundation (Social Sciences Small Grants Scheme) which contributed to the cost of research for this book and to Patricia King who typed the manuscript and prepared the whole volume for publication.

J.R. FREARS   JEAN-LUC PARODI

CONTENTS

TABLES

ABBREVIATIONS

CD	*Centre Démocrate* (part of *Réformateurs*, 1973)
CDS	*Centre des Démocrates Sociaux* (part of UDF)
CDP	*Centre pour la Démocratie et le Progrès*
CERES	*Centre d'étude et de recherche socialistes* (left-wing of PS)
CFDT	*Confédération française démocratique du Travail*
CGT	*Confédération générale du Travail*
CNIP	*Centre nationale des Indépendents et des Paysans*
DC	*Démocratie Chrétienne*
FA	*Front autogestionnaire*
FGDS	*Fédération de la Gauche démocrate et socialiste* (Socialist-Radical alliance 1965-69)
LCR	*Ligue communiste révolutionnaire*
LO	*Lutte ouvrière*
MDSF	*Mouvement démocrate socialiste de France*
MRG	*Mouvement des Radicaux de gauche* (left-Radicals)
MRP	*Mouvement républicain populaire*
PCF	*Parti communiste français*
PR	*Parti républicain* (formerly RI, part of UDF)
PS	*Parti socialiste*
PSD	*Parti socialiste démocrate*
PSU	*Parti socialiste unifié*
Rad	Radical Party (part of *Réformateurs* 1973; part of UDF 1978)
Ref	*Mouvement Réformateur*
RI	*Républicains Indépendents* (*Giscardiens* 1962-77, now PR)
RPF	*Rassemblement du Peuple français* (Gaullism 1947-53)
RPR	*Rassemblement pour la République*
SFIO	*Section française de l'internationale ouvrière* (Socialist Party 1905-69)
UDF	*Union pour la Démocratie française*
UDR	*Union des Démocrates pour la République* (Gaullism 1968-76)
UGSD	*Union de la Gauche socialiste et démocrate* (Socialist-MRG alliance 1973)

CHAPTER 1. INTRODUCTION

War will not take place

In Jean Giraudoux's play 'The Trojan War will not take place'[1], a
little good sense could have averted that long and bitter conflict. Unfortunately fate, and some of the sillier members of
the Trojan and Greek political elites, decreed otherwise. Political conflict in France, as illustrated by the interesting elections of March 1978, presents some parallels.

There is nothing in contemporary French society, no rooted
economic discontent, no implacable separatist loyalties to church
or region, no oppressed minority, which allows one to regard conflict as inevitable. There is no significant social group which
challenges the legitimacy of the Fifth Republic as a regime. The
1978 elections took place in an atmosphere of almost total calm
and peacefulness. People voted respectfully and gratefully for
their local political notables. President and Prime Minister
alike bathed benignly in their recovered popularity. They asked
the voters to make the 'right choice' based on good sense. The
voters did as they were asked. Yet the whole electoral contest
was presented as a *choix de société*, a choice between two radi-
cally different visions of how society should be organised, a
life-and death struggle between freedom and servitude. The
Communist Party, even if partially victorious as the junior part-
nar of the left-wing coalition, would, it was argued, employ its
super-human powers of organisation, resolve, and treachery to turn
France into a replica of Eastern Europe's Peoples' Democracies.
Although most pro-government campaigning stressed the dire consequences of a victory of the left, and most Communist campaigning
emphasised the same theme - yes, society really would change once
there were Communist ministers in the government - nobody seemed
to pause and reflect that in a well-established democracy abrupt
and fundamental change very seldom comes from the ballot box or

from anywhere else for that matter. In other words if the left
had won the election, the first thing President Giscard d'Estaing
could have said to François Mitterrand is 'war will not take
place'. As we suggest in chapter 8, there is very little evidence
to suggest that the worst predictions of both right and left
would have come about: defence secrets leaked to the Russians or
coup d'état by the French military, wholesale nationalisation or
economic sabotage by capitalists, the establishment of the
machinery for a totalitarian police state or administrative
counter-revolution by the servants of the state. In a democracy
governments cannot stray outside what is acceptable to public
opinion. It is hard to see that fundamental changes would have
been acceptable to a basically contented and affluent consumer
society. At all events the experiment with a government of the
left, the first coalition of its kind in France since 1936, the
first partially Communist government in the history of the European Communists, would, in all probability, not have lasted long.
Communists and Socialists gave ample warning of their determination not to agree, and the date of the next election was at the
sole discretion of the President of the Republic, who would be
looking for just the right opportunity to let the electors bring
the experiment to an end. So there was no need for war to take
place. It seems to us that French democracy is more solid and
sensible than much of the French political elite gives it credit
for being. In Giraudoux's play Cassandra correctly foretells that
human stupidity would prevail and insist upon self-destruction.
After almost a quarter century of recovered prosperity, political
stability, and legitimacy, however, the French are perfectly
capable, whoever wins the next election, of declaring, like Hector
and Andromaque, 'war will not take place'. Any conflict that
should then occur will, like the war of Troy, be an unnecessary one.

Elections in the Fifth Republic

In March for the third time in the 1970's at a national election the choice was presented as a *choix de société*. In the 1960's

it was otherwise. Then the choice was more personalised and tangible: for or against de Gaulle and his blend of historic resonance, strong government, and national self-assertion. From 1958 to 1968 the nation supported de Gaulle in four parliamentary elections, one Presidential election, and four referenda. Then in April 1969 it rejected his referendum on Senate and regional reform and he was gone. Two months later Georges Pompidou was elected on the slogan *continuité et ouverture* - continuity of the Fifth Republic and its institutions for which de Gaulle had won acceptance, an opening towards new men, a more cooperative foreign policy, and a less authoritarian style.

In the early 1970's the parties of the left - Communists, Socialists, and some of the Radicals - to whom it had been clear for some years that divided they could make no impact whatsoever on Gaullism's dominance of the state - renewed their efforts to present a united front. The new Socialist Party, wider in its appeal and more dynamic than the old SFIO, led by François Mitterrand, an important national figure and deeply committed to the strategy of an alliance of all the left ever since his presidential candidature against de Gaulle in 1965, joined forced with a Communist Party (PCF) that seemed ready for change. Since the mid-1960's, the Communist leadership had moved towards some understanding that attachment to the unacceptable was no way to win power in a democratic country. The movement was uncertain at times and encountered set-backs. For instance the crushing by Brezhnev in 1968 of 'Socialism with a human face' in Czechoslovakia, though initially condemned by the PCF, was mirrored by a recrudescence of intolerance and orthodoxy in the French party. Nonetheless in June 1972 Socialists, Communists, and the so-called left-Radicals signed the celebrated *programme commun* - the joint manifesto for a government of the left the up-dating of which was to cause such bitter animosity in the summer of 1977. So in the Parliamentary elections of March 1973 the principal issue was this choice: do you want a government of the left that includes Communists? Another issue, discussed at great length, was the constitutional uncertainty of a situation in which the country might have a President elected on one set of policies and a National Assembly, which has the power to censure and bring down a government appointed by the President, elected upon another contradictory set. Despite the threats that constitutional crisis and totalitarian collectivism would follow a victory of the left, the left made considerable gains compared with its low-tide of the 1968 election. However the President's supporters - the *majorité* composed of Gaullists, *Giscardiens*, and some centrists who had been in opposition under de Gaulle - comfortably won a keenly-fought election in which public interest and participation had been very high.

In 1974, following the sudden death of President Pompidou in April, the second national contest to be presented as a *choix de société* occurred. The second ballot, the gladiatorial single combat which has done so much to reinforce the trends in the Fifth Republic towards a bi-polar party structure, was contested by Valéry Giscard d'Estaing and the Socialist leader Mitterrand. Actually the invocations of chaos and communism were less strident than in the parliamentary elections either of 1973 or of 1978, although the effects of the Presidency passing to the left would have been more profound. Had Mitterrand won, his presidential powers might easily have found the reinforcement of a parliamentary majority secured at an early and well-timed dissolution. He very nearly did win but, in the highest poll in the history of universal suffrage in France - almost 88%, Giscard d'Estaing was elected with just 50.7% of the votes cast.

With the election of Giscard d'Estaing begins the story of the 1978 Parliamentary elections. The new President had absorbed into his *majorité* all that remained of the old centrist opposition - Jean Lecanuet and his friends of the *Centre Démocrate*, Jean-Jacques Servan-Schreiber and his friends of the old Radical Party and the Centre-Left. The dominance of Gaullism, either in the orthodox form of the early years of the Fifth Republic or in the pragmatic technocratic form of the Pompidou era, was over. Giscard d'Estaing, though he had served in Gaullist governments and supported the Fifth Republic and its institutions as envisaged by de Gaulle, was not of the Gaullist clan, and he had defeated the official Gaullist candidate for the Presidency, Jacques Chaban-Delmas. That he was helped to do so by Jacques Chirac, who

TABLE 1.1   PARLIAMENTARY ELECTIONS (*ELECTIONS LEGISLATIVES*) IN THE FIFTH REPUBLIC

(% 1st ballot vote - metropolitan France only; National Assembly seats - metropolitan and overseas)

	Oct 1958		Nov 1962		March 1967		June 1968		March 1973		March 1978	
	%	seats	%	seats	%	seats	%	seats	%	seats	%	seats
Abstentions (% of electorate)	22.9		31.3		18.9		20.0		18.7		16.6	
Left:												
Communists (PCF)	19.2	.10	21.7	41	22.5	73	20.0	34	21.4	73	20.7	86
SFIO (Socialist Party pre-1969)	15.7	44	12.6	66	19.0	116	16.5	57	20.8	101	25.0	114
Socialist/Radical alliances FGDS (1967-8); UGSD 1973; PS/MRG 1978												
Radicals	8.3	32	7.8	39								
PSU, Extreme Left, Other Left			2.4	-	2.1	4	4.7	-	3.6	2	3.6	-
(Total Left)	(43.2)	(86)	(44.5)	(146)	(43.6)	(193)	(41.2)	(91)	(45.8)	(176)	(49.3)	(200)
Centre												
MRP	11.1	57	9.1)									
Independents	22.9	133	7.7)	55								
Opposition Centre (CD/PDM)					13.4	41	10.3	33				
Réformateurs (CD + Rad, 1973)									13.1	34		
Majorité												
CDP (Pro-*majorité* centrists,1973)										30		
UDF (*Giscardiens* + centre, 1978)											21.4	137
RI (*Giscardiens* pre-1978)			5.9	35	37.7	(44	44.7	(64	36.0	(55		
Gaullists	19.5	199	31.9	233		(201		(296		(183	22.5	150
Other *majorité*									0.7	5	2.0	3
(Total *Majorité*)			(37.8)	(268)	(37.7)	(245)	(44.7)	(360)	(36.7)	(273)	(45.9)	(290)
Other	3.3		8.6	13	5.4	8	3.5	3	4.4	7	4.8*	1

* includes 'Ecologists' - 2.1%

TABLE 1.2   PRESIDENTIAL ELECTIONS IN THE FIFTH REPUBLIC (% of votes cast, metropolitan France only)

December 1965

	Candidate	1st ballot m votes	1st ballot %	2nd ballot m votes	2nd ballot %
Abstentions (% of electorate)		15.0		15.5	
Majorité	de Gaulle	10.4	43.7	12.6	54.5
Opposition Centre	Lecanuet	3.8	15.8		
Left	Mitterrand	7.7	32.2	10.6	45.5
Extreme Left					
Extreme Right	Tixier-Vignancour	1.3	5.3		
Others	Marcilhacy	0.4	1.7		
	Barbu	0.3	1.2		

June 1969

	Candidate	1st ballot m votes	1st ballot %	2nd ballot m votes	2nd ballot %
Abstentions (% of electorate)		21.8		30.9	
Majorité	Pompidou	9.8	44.0	10.7	57.6
Opposition Centre	Poher	5.2	23.4	7.9	42.4
Left	Defferre (PS)	1.1	5.1		
	Rocard (PSU)	0.8	3.7		
	Duclos (PCF)	4.8	21.5		
Extreme Left	Krivine	0.2	1.1		
Others	Ducatel	0.3	1.1		

May 1974

	Candidate	1st ballot m votes	1st ballot %	2nd ballot m votes	2nd ballot %
Abstentions (% of electorate)		15.1		12.1	
Majorité	Chaban-Delmas	3.6	14.6		
	Royer	0.8	3.2		
	Giscard d'Estaing	8.3	32.9	13.1	50.7
Left	Mitterrand	10.9	43.4	12.7	49.3
Extreme Left	Krivine	0.1	0.4		
	Laguiller	0.6	2.4		
Extreme Right	Le Pen	0.2	0.8		
Others	Dumont (ecol)	0.3	1.3		
	Muller	0.2	0.7		
	Renouvin	0.04	0.2		
	Sebag	0.04	0.2		
	Héraud	0.02	0.1		

6

subsequently and rapidly became the undisputed leader of the
Gaullist movement, and the most vigorous and determined opponent -
even rival - of the President within the ranks of the *majorité* is
one of the most curious elements of the tale of conflicts between
allies that characterised the 1978 election and which will be
discussed in the next chapter. On the left, the harmony and the
low Communist profile that characterised the 1974 Presidential
election, so nearly crowned with victory, was replaced in 1977,
for reasons that will also be discussed in the next chapter, by
ferocious enmity of a quite suicidal nature.

The whole of the first four years of the Giscard d'Estaing
Presidency were dominated by the approach of the 1978 elections.
Should they be precipitated by an early dissolution of Parliament?
Should government policy favour those most likely to support it
at election? On both these questions the President said no
whereas his Prime Minister Jacques Chirac said yes, thereby re-
vealing himself to be of inferior judgement. Every electoral
contest, local elections, parliamentary by-elections, even every
local by-election, was scrutinised like the entrails of a chicken
for some augury for 1978.

Parliamentary by-elections are not a very regular occurrence
in France because a deputy is always elected with a *suppléant* who
stands in for him in his Parliamentary seat if he becomes dis-
qualified - either through death or through acceptance of ministerial or other public office - to continue as deputy. They occur
either through the original election being declared invalid (one
in metropolitan France between 1973 and 1978), through the resignation of a member (1), through the death of a *suppléant* who
has already been called upon to sit as *député* (2) or, the most
common cause of by-elections, through the desire of a dismissed
minister, after a government re-shuffle, to regain his parliamentary seat. In such cases (14) the *suppléant* obligingly resigns
the seat and a by-election occurs. As Table 1.3 shows the left
made considerable gains at almost all these by-elections. Four
seats were won and only the two ex-Prime Ministers Messmer and
Chirac prevented the left from gaining votes. A factor which

TABLE 1.3

BY-ELECTIONS (*ELECTIONS PARTIELLES*) - 1973-78 (metropolitan France only)
(Names indicate a minister or ex-minister seeking to recover his seat which his ministerial functions had obliged him, under Art. 23 of the constitution, to give up to his *suppléant*)

THE LEFT -

CHANGE FROM 1973

(% POINTS - 1st ballot)

	PS/MRG	PCF	Total Left (inc. extr. left)	ADDITIONAL GAINS AT 2ND BALLOT
Landes 1 (1973)	+15*	-0	+15	+3[++]
Ardèche 2 (1974) - Torre	+11*	-3	+10	+1
Côte d'Or (1974) - Lecat	+13*	-4	+11	+1
Dordogne 1 (1974) - Guêna	+ 3	+3*	+ 5	-5
Loire-Atl. 7 (1974) - Guichard	+13	-2	+12	
Moselle 8 (1974) - Messmer	+ 1	-1	+ 0	
Rhône 10 (1974) - Ducray	+15*	-3	+11	+5[++]
Savoie 2 (1974) - Fontanet	+11**	+0	+12	+1[++]
Seine-Maritime 6 (1975)	+ 4	+4*	+ 4	-2
Vienne 2 (1975) - Abelin	+ 8**	-2	+ 7	+2
Tarn 2 (1975) - Limouzy	+ 8	-1	+ 3	
Indre et Loire (1976) - Royer	+ 4	-1	+ 1	
Hte-Loire 2 (1976)	+ 2*	-2	+ 2	-0[++]
Allier 4 (1976) - Péronnet	+11	+1*	+12	+3
Corrèze 3 (1976) - Chirac	+ 2	-6	- 2	
Gironde 5 (1976) - Achille Fould	+12*	-4	+ 9	-0
Paris 3 (1976) - Tibéri	+ 4	-4	- 5	
Yvelines 5 (1976) - Destremau	+ 6	+4*	+ 8	+1
Average gain or loss	+8	-1	+6	+1

*   Candidate in second ballot
**   Socialist candidates who supplanted Communists to reach second ballot
++   Seat gained by left.

became a bone of contention in the growing discord between Communists and Socialists emerges clearly from this table. The Socialists in all cases made gains, sometimes spectacular, occasionally ousting their Communist partners from local leadership of the left. In almost all cases the Communists made losses compared with 1973. Furthermore where a Socialist became the sole candidate of the left at the second ballot, further gains in votes were made. Where the candidate was a Communist, first ballot strength was lost in 2 out of 3 cases. In Dordogne the left had had 53% of the first ballot vote but had failed to win the seat at the second.

In local elections the story was similar. In the 1976 cantonal elections for the *Conseils Généraux* in the *Départements*, the first nationwide test of opinion since the Presidential election, the left reached almost 53% of the first ballot vote - a level that subsequently turned out to have been the apogee of its electoral progress. President Giscard d'Estaing later admitted that this was the most demoralising moment for his supporters.[2] It was followed by confusion in the *majorité* and not long after by the departure of Jacques Chirac from the government. Once again the Socialists had been the principal beneficiaries and had eliminated some Communists by running ahead of them at the first ballot. The municipal elections of March 1977 were dominated by the rivalry within the *majorité* between Chirac and Michel d'Ornano, who was clearly the nominee of the President and Prime Minister Raymond Barre, to become the first Mayor of Paris since 1870. Chirac won. Although this rivalry was largely confined to Paris, the left appeared to be much less divided. It presented united lists in most cities and fought a united election - any conflicts over the composition of joint lists having been settled earlier. The left won control of 159 out of 221 cities with a population over 30,000 (a gain of 56 from 1971). 72 had Communist mayors (+27) and 83 had Socialist or left-Radical mayors (+43). Many of the more spectacular gains were in cities in strongly Catholic regions where the left had always been weak - Rennes, Angers, or Reims for instance.

The growth of the left throughout the 1970's, especially in the larger towns, right up to the local elections of spring 1977 is illustrated by Table 1.4.

Table 1.4   Votes for the left in Cities over 30,000 population
(221 cities)

	% of vote
Municipal elections 1971 - 1st ballot	46.9*
Parliamentary elections 1973 - 1st ballot	48.0
Presidential elections 1974 - 2nd ballot	50.2
Municipal elections 1977 - 1st ballot	51.0

* includes lists led by PCF, PSU, PS, or MRG - though some
such lists included Centrists.

(Source: J-L Parodi, 'Après les elections municipales: la fin de
la transition?', Revue Politique et Parlementaire, mai 1977)

That things began to go better for the *majorité* in the latter half of 1977 is undoubtedly due to the furious rivalry and hostility, to be discussed in the next chapter, that broke out between Communists and Socialists. There is however, it should be noted, a school of thought which held that success at local elections was not a pointer to success at a national election because the character of the regime was not at stake in local elections or even because there is a perceived division of roles where the left is considered suitable for local but not for national government[3]. The left remained ahead in the opinion polls of voting intentions right up to the eve of the elections in March 1978, though, in response to the question 'in your heart of hearts' (*au fond de vous-même*) 'who do you want to win the election?', the *majorité* was consistently in the lead![4]

The Electoral System

The elections of March 1978 took place on the curious two
ballot simple majority system, unique to France though somewhat
modified since the previous contest in 1973. The country is
divided into 491 constituencies (1 more than in 1973) - of which
17 are in overseas Départements or Territories like the island
of Martinique in the Caribbean or French Polynesia in the Pacific.
The division is somewhat unequal: St. Pierre et Miquelon, an
island off Canada, has one deputy for 4,000 electors, while at
Martigues in the South of France, there is one for 168,000. For
the 474 constituencies of Metropolitan France, to which all the
figures in this book refer, the average is 73,000. The most important change since 1974 was the enfranchisement of the 18-21 year-
old age group, as promised by President Giscard d'Estaing during
his election campaign. This, together with normal population
growth, had added 4½ million voters to the register in 1978.
Another change in the electoral law, supported by all parties,
made it easier for French citizens living abroad to vote. However this included the curious disposition whereby these overseas
residents could register in any town of over 30,000 population
in any constituency whether they had any connection with it or
not. Many of these electors registered in marginal constituencies
and a major scandal developed over the suggestion that French
diplomatic missions abroad in countries like the Ivory Coast were
carrying out systematic registrations of proxy votes on behalf
of the *majorité* in sensitive constituencies. The Socialist deputy
for Montpellier, Georges Frèche, probably owes his defeat to the
exceptional number of overseas proxy votes in that city. François
Mitterrand called the affair a 'veritable racket' and raised it
with the President of the Republic in their post-electoral
meeting.

For a deposit of 1,000 Fr ($200) (repayable, together with
certain election printing expenses, if a threshold of 5% of votes
cast is attained) any elector can be a candidate. A candidate
receiving the absolute majority (50% + 1) of votes cast in his

constituency is elected at the first ballot[5]. If no candidate
finds himself in this happy position, a second ballot is held a
week later on the following Sunday. No new candidate may register
at the second ballot. Candidates may contest the second provided
they have obtained at the first the support of at least 12½% of
the registered electorate[6]. This bar, raised from 10% at the previous election, meant that all candidates of the left were eliminated from 8 constituencies where a second ballot took place,
and all candidates of the *majorité* from 5. In most of such cases
the second ballot, by virtue of alliances, consisted of just one
candidate - elected with 100% of those who bothered to turn out.
Most second ballot contests, however, turn out to be duels - not
because all but two candidates have been eliminated but because
of the system of alliances both on the left and within the
majorité. The parties of the left have agreed at every election
since 1962, although the PCF refused to commit itself in advance
of the 1978 election, that only one candidate of the left shall
remain at the second ballot and that it shall be he who scored
most votes at the first. The *majorité*, which used to present a
single candidate in most constituencies, now has a similar
arrangement to the left. In 1978 there were 'primaries' between
the two principal formations of the *majorité* - the Gaullist RPR
(*Rassemblement pour la République*) and the *Giscardien*-Centrist
UDF (Union for French Democracy) in 352 of the 474 metropolitan
constituencies. All in all 4268 candidates, a record - almost 9
per constituency, two-thirds of whom would be eliminated by the
12% rule after the first ballot - joined battle when the campaign
at last was officially open.

NOTES

(1) La guerre de Troie n'aura pas lieu, Paris, Grasset, 1935.

(2) L'Express, 9-15 mai, 1977.

(3) G. Lavau in an unpublished paper, Conference on 'Two Decades of Gaullism', Brockport, N.Y., June 1978.

(4) See below p.29.

(5) Unless turnout is very small and he has received the votes of less than one-quarter of the registered electors.

(6) If only one candidate reaches this bar, the candidate who comes second may also proceed to the second ballot if he chooses to do so.

LES RÉGIONS EN FRANCE

Source : D.A.T.A.R. 1975

CHAPTER 2. POLITICAL FORCES ON THE EVE OF THE ELECTION

It has become a commonplace of the analysis of French
political life to comment upon the bi-polarity of political parties in the Fifth Republic. The fragmented multi-party system of
earlier Republics, which included a wide spectrum of small groups
and independents almost totally unimpeded by the notion of party
discipline or electoral engagements from making any sort of coalition as often as they liked, has gradually changed since 1958
into a system of two rival and relatively cohesive blocs - the
left and the *majorité*. It was the appeal and the success of
Gaullism, combined with an electoral system that favoured large
parties or cohesive alliances, that brought about this change.
The public support given massively to General de Gaulle in 1958
for the establishment of a new Republic with a stronger executive
leadership based upon a strong Presidency, given also to the party UNR (Union for a New Republic) formed to back de Gaulle and the
new political institutions, given also in 1962 to the all-impor-
tant notion of a directly-elected Presidency, transformed French
political life. Independents and Centrists, like the old MRP,
who tried to resist the growing Presidentialism in 1962 were
crushed at the November elections as their voters joined the ranks
of Gaullism. Throughout the 1960's innovation and progress were
synonymous with Gaullism. The parties of the left continued to
decline - the old Socialist SFIO and the Radicals appeared as a
dwindling and uninspiring band of ageing fixers, the Communists
as irrelevant Stalinists. However, from the first timid electoral
pact of 1962, the parties of the left began to realise that they
could only resist perpetual defeat by Gaullism if they united
their efforts. François Mitterrand's presidential candidature in
1965, his leadership of the FGDS (a federation of Socialists and
Radicals), his promotion of an FGDS-PCF electoral pact in 1967,
the signature by both groups of a common declaration in February
1968, all culminated, after some severe setbacks in the years

15

1968-1971, to the signature of the *Programme Commun* in June 1972.
From 1973 to 1977 the *Union de la Gauche* was at its most successful electorally. The Communists played their full part in this
process. They redoubled their criticisms of persecution in the
Soviet Union in order to indicate their lessening attachment to
that regime. They declared that the Soviet regime was no longer
a model for the socialism they had in mind in France. They
dropped, at their 22nd Congress in 1976, the Leninist notion of
Dictatorship of the Proletariat from their objectives. A cohesive
and united left, so it appeared, would face the electorate in
1978 with credible and acceptable aims.

In the meantime, as we observed in the last chapter, successive Presidents of the Republic had attracted into the *majorité*
camp what remained of the opposition centre. So the party system
by the mid-1970's presented the picture not of a two-party system
but of two relatively cohesive rival blocs. The *majorité* consisted of Gaullists (called RPR since 1976), *Giscardiens* (PR -
Republican Party - since 1977), those Radicals who, under the
somewhat erratic leadership of Jean-Jacques Servan-Schreiber, refused alliance with the Communists, and the CDS, the Centre of
Social Democrats which, led by Lecanuet, had re-united in 1976
the different fragments of the basically Christian Democratic
Centre that had split away at various times from the opposition
to join the *majorité*. The components of the *Union de la Gauche*
were the Socialist Party (PS), the Left-Radicals (MRG), and the
Communists. The PS, successfully relaunched under the leadership
of François Mitterrand at the Epinay Congress in 1971, had grown
by the addition of a part of the PSU (United Socialist Party) led
by Michel Rocard in 1974 and the support of France's second-
largest Union federation the CFDT. Socialists and MRG, that frag-
ment of the old Radical Party who for ideological and electoral
reasons, preferred to stick with the left, had had a pact in 1973
within the *Union de la Gauche* for joint candidatures. All that
remained outside the two big blocs were a handful of *groupuscules*
on the extreme left, revolutionary and anarchist, fragments of the
extreme right, the ecologists and Michel Jobert, President Pompidou's
last Foreign Minister, with his *Mouvement Démocrate*.

The role of Presidential elections in the changing structure of the party system is quintessential. The support for each new President in his election campaign has defined the boundaries of the new *majorité*. The constitutional requirement that only the two candidates most successful at the first ballot may contest the second imparts a bi-polar championship style to the election. It leaves the winner President of the Republic and leader of the Executive and gives to the loser, in the case of François Mitterrand at any rate, the status in the public eye of leader of the opposition. Finally, though this has since 1974 become an instrument of a new fragmentation rather than re-unification, a credible Presidential candidate has become the basic requirement for a successful political party. The ascendancy of de Gaulle and Pompidou were the years of the ascendancy of the Gaullist party. The rising star of Giscard d'Estaing has been the impetus for the growth of a Centrist-*Giscardien* movement. The rising star of Mitterrand has been the impetus for the growth of the PS. The RPR operation and the rivalry within the *majorité* stems from the Gaullist need to launch Chirac as a credible Presidential candidate. The gnashing of teeth from the Communists is explicable in part by the fact that they have no credible candidate nor any chance of winning the Presidency - though they have announced their intention to present a candidate in 1981.

This new tendency towards rivalry and division within both camps succeeds a period of some fifteen years characterised by a growing cohesiveness and represents the most important recent development in the party system. Bi-polarity in the system as a whole has been supplemented by bi-polarity within each camp. Each element within each camp has acted defensively to protect itself against domination and eclipse by its partner. The *Giscardiens* and Centrists have grouped together to end the domination of the Gaullists. The RPR's aggressive tone is a defensive reflex against the fear of eclipse by the *Giscardiens*. The Socialists and MRG have acted to ensure the left would not be dominated by the Communists. The PCF's extraordinary hostility towards the Socialists in the crucial pre-electoral period was in defence of their electoral fortresses against the appeal of the Socialists, in

defence of their leading role as a working-class movement, and in
fear of being a dominated and junior partner in a government of
the left. The remainder of this chapter will analyse the conflicts within each camp which were vital to the outcome of the
election, and important for the future of the party system.

a. The dis-union of the left

The constraints of the electoral system and the efforts of
party leaders had gradually, over ten years or so, built the
Union of the Left. It was however an alliance with a problem
somewhat unusual in party systems: each party felt the need to
stress simultaneously both unity and the difference between them.[1]

The two partners, the Communist Party and the Socialist
Party, from those first tentative steps towards union in 1962-65,
gave their alliance the substance of an electoral pact from 1966
to 1971, endowed it in 1972 with an actual programme of government, and extended it to cover local government in the elections
of 1976 and 1977. With the Mitterrand presidential candidature
of 1974 and the presentation in almost all large towns of joint
lists in the 1977 municipal elections, this electoral alliance had
in effect led to the temporary disappearance from the scene of
both partners and the replacement of two distinct parties each
with their own separate image by a united front. It seemed natural,
therefore, after twelve years, of an alliance that, except for the
setback at the end of the 1960's had continued to grow stronger,
the most salient characteristics of each partner would have become
progressively less marked or even have disappeared. By allying
itself with the PCF, the PS was able to demonstrate its solid
commitment to the left and to reinforce its image as a partisan
of social change. By allying itself with the PS, the PCF was able
to free itself to some extent from its image as a Stalinist party
belonging outside the normal political system. Thus the rough
edges in the appeal of both parties were smoothed by their commitment to the *Union de la Gauche* and the left as a whole felt the
benefit.

From the individual point of view of each party, however,
there remained a slight difficulty. There was no question of a

merger between them - of 'wiping out 1920' as Guy Mollet used to put it - and so each party was bound to think about its own continued existence and therefore of the advantages it might gain from the alliance. In short, what was the best way for each, within the alliance, to compete successfully with the other?

It might have been supposed that the electoral profit which alliance had earned for the left in 1973 and 1974, as well as at by-elections and local elections since, would have been equally shared. This was not so - and when opinion polls, especially after the 1974 Presidential election, began to show the differences between the Communist and Socialist electorates becoming blurred, it is not surprising that both partners, especially the PCF, felt the need to stress their individual and separate identities.

Stressing differences, however, in a competitive situation means, naturally enough, stressing in what way one is superior to one's rival and therefore, directly or indirectly, implicitly or explicitly, emphasising the rival's deficiencies. Thus, within the country's bi-polar party system of two big alliances, there re-emerged the old struggle for the leadership of the left - a struggle which a two-ballot electoral system of course permits. This dialectic of unity and difference is by no means independent of the electoral calendar. It demands of each partner an adroit management of time so that unity is the order of the day in election periods and difference can be stressed in the spaces between.

It is in this perspective that the breakdown of negotiations over the updating of the *programme commun* on 22 September, 1977 must be seen. For the PCF, joint signatures on a revised *programme commun* would have been putting the accent on union a little too early. For the Socialists one possibility, with some advantages from their point of view, would have been a *programme commun* supplemented by a list of points on which the two parties continued to disagree. Such a solution, however, would have allowed the PCF to make these policy differences its main campaign theme and this the PS could not accept. The breakdown of September 22nd thus placed both partners in a difficult situation which seems neither to have been planned nor even to have been foreseen.

Cornered into division, each knowing that it could not take the responsibility at the election for breaking the alliance and its joint programme, the two parties of the left for the next six months engaged in the most violent hostilities either had known in the Fifth Republic. Paradoxically this setback in a process of union which had developed so greatly over the years was experienced as a much greater crisis for the left than anything that had happened in the days of paper-thin electoral alliances, with no manifesto, in 1967 and 1968.

PCF strategy - in as far as a series of contrasting styles of behaviour and of frequently contradictory speeches can be called a strategy - seems to have been based during these six months on a conviction that the PS would be compelled to concede or face collapse. So a tremendous campaign was undertaken in order to show that the PS had 'veered to the right' and the invective in L'Humanité returned to its most Stalinist form. Since the principal objective was to win back Communist voters who might have been tempted to vote Socialist, it was important to refuse any *rapprochement*. When, for instance, François Mitterrand in early 1978 accepted the Communist proposal (which he had refused until then), for an increase in the national minimum wage (SMIC) to 2400 francs a month, the gesture was treated with contempt by the PCF - a clear indication that it still regarded difference as more important than union. The Communist Party threw all the weight it could command into the anti-Socialist battle. The CGT was brought in to the fray with direct attacks on Socialist attitudes and policies, and its Secretary-General Georges Séguy publicly took part with Marchais in big Communist election rallies. Curiously enough, as the first ballot drew nearer, the PCF suddenly seized upon some conciliatory proposals by the pro-Socialist union CFDT as a point of departure for possible agreement - a move not calculated to delight the loyal CGT.

To compel the PS to accept Communist terms for a cease-fire, the PCF even went so far as to cast doubt on the old notion of 'republican discipline' - *désistement réciproque* or the fundamental principle of presenting only one candidate of the left in each constituency at the second ballot for all to support. Without

désistement réciproque the left would be annihilated at the second
ballot, and yet Georges Marchais and his party actually went so
far as to hint that the decision to withdraw Communist candidates
at the second ballot might depend on how the Party did at the
first. These two themes, contempt for 'republican discipline' and
the possibility of not withdrawing Communist candidates, were badly received by public opinion and party workers and were not developed - but they were not dropped either. As time passed and it
became clear that the PS would neither concede nor collapse, the
approach of polling-day demanded that the priority accorded up to
then to difference, should now be accorded to the concept of union.
The Communist campaign at the end switched to union - the appeal
for a 'good agreement on the 13th March' (the day after the first
ballot) to ensure, according to it, 'victory on the 19th'.

The PS, in response to this prolonged anti-Socialist offen-
sive, did nothing in particular but, with an air of stoic resignation, simply waited for the storm to blow itself out. The main
thing was to say nothing and do nothing that the Communists could
use to support their accusations. Socialist speeches became
almost entirely defensive, directed towards supporters of the left
rather than towards the undecided floating voters whose support
it was necessary to gain. Any counter-attack that was made
focussed on the PCF's lack of good faith (for instance in not
accepting Mitterrand's olive branch over the minimum wage) or on
what were supposed to be its true motives - and here discreet
reference was made to the uncompleted process of 'desovietisation'.
Finally the PS accused its partner of breaking up the union of the
left and questioned it constantly about the second ballot, declaring for its part that Socialists, whatever happened, would hon-
our the agreement to stand aside for Communist candidates who in
any constituency got more votes than they.

All available evidence (Table 2.1) points to a strong
desire by supporters of the left for union. They wanted it before
the breakdown of September 22nd. Disagreement between the parties
distressed them. Reconciliation was what they hoped for. They
were reluctant to believe that it was Mitterrand, the very symbol
of union in his 1974 campaign, who had deserted them.

TABLE 2.1   Opinion polls and the breakdown of the *Union de la Gauche*.

		All Electors %	supporters of:- PCF %	PS %
a. Do you want the left to reach agreement?				
(Sept. 1-3)	Yes	47	88	75
	No	24	3	11
	No opinion	29	9	14
b. Parties of the left are in disagreement: are you				
(30 Sept. - 4 Oct.)	Pleased?	33	6	18
	Unhappy?	41	87	66
	No opinion	24	7	16
c. Do you hope disagreement can be resolved?				
(30 Sept. - 4 Oct.)	Yes	46	90	70
	No	34	5	22
	No opinion	20	5	10
d. Do you consider François Mitterrand to be a sincere Socialist?				
	Yes	59	43	81
	No	21	46	7
	No opinion	20	15	12
attached to Union of the Left?				
(4-8 Oct)	Yes	47	40	65
	No	29	39	18
	No opinion	24	21	17

(Source: SOFRES)

There is unfortunately what one might call a 'dynamic of disunion'. Even in periods when union is more to the fore than difference, a floating segment of the Socialist vote continues to find the idea of voting Communist at the second ballot deeply objectionable and in its heart of hearts hopes the *majorité* will win the election. Table 2.1 illustrated the hopes for unity but it also contains some troubling indicators for the left: 11% of Socialist supporters wanted no agreement in September, 18% were quite happy with the breakdown, and 22% wanted no new agreement. Table 2.3 shows how the number of electors hoping 'in their heart of hearts' that the left would win was less than the number expressing the intention of voting for the left. This particular form of hesitation probably affected as many as one Socialist supporter in six. Finally in chapter 6 (Table 6.7) we shall see the confirmation of the trend presaged in pre-election opinion polls that one-third of Socialist first ballot voters would not be prepared to vote Communist at the second.

And so, for the first time since 1962, Communists and Socialists entered the first ballot in a state of disunion and mutual antagonism, to the great confusion of public opinion.

b. The *Majorité*: territorial rivalries

The fissures on the left are much deeper than those in the *majorité*. On the left, at the level of political elites at any rate, they involve two different ideological frameworks, two different visions of society and the world. There are deep differences over the attachment to the norms of liberal democracy. In addition the PCF is in the agonising throes of a change, which would involve the loss of its identity as a Communist Party, yet to which there is no viable alternative if it wishes to have any part in governing a democratic country.

On the right such wars as there are, like those between animals or birds or the Mafia, are more about territory than belief. The Presidency, the size of rival Parliamentary groups, candidatures in good constituencies, ministerial portfolios, chairmanships of committees - these are the things Gaullists and *Giscardiens* fight about. There are differences of style of course between the

ranting populism of Chirac and the urbane liberalism of Giscard
d'Estaing. These differences in style involve some differences
in belief - about how much one should tolerate opposition for
instance. There are very few real differences of policy. There
are some make-believe differences which are not particularly important. President Giscard d'Estaing and his friends are, in rhetoric
at any rate, more favourable to European integration than the
Chiraquiens. We were informed, however, by a leading Gaullist
(admittedly in the honeymoon days of the Chirac premiership) that
Giscard d'Estaing, by initiating regular summit meetings of EEC
Heads of Government, had done more to advance de Gaulle's notion
of *l'Europe des patries* than any orthodox Gaullist. On defence
and foreign policy Gaullists are supposed to be more fiercely in
favour of 'national independence'. While perhaps giving more
emphasis to good relations with the Americans, the President in
all important areas has fully identified himself with the foreign
and defence policies of his predecessors. *Giscardiens* are supposed
to be less interventionist in economic affairs than the Gaullists,
but a President, trained at both the National School of Administration and the Polytéchnique, a Minister of Finance under Presidents
de Gaulle and Pompidou, is no stranger to state-direction of the
economy.

On other levels *Giscardiens* and Gaullists are closely bound
together. They have been ministers in each other's governments.
They have been members of each other's ministerial *cabinets, sup-
pléants* to each other's Parliamentarians. The newly-elected
Chiraquien deputy for the Vosges, Philippe Séguin, for instance
was a member of Raymond Barre's personal *cabinet*, and Bertrand de
Maigret, a national secretary of the *Giscardien* Republican Party,
was *suppléant* for a Gaullist deputy in the last Parliament. Sometimes they contest the elections as candidates of one component of
the *majorité* and take their seats in the National Assembly as a
deputy of the other. Such was the case of Frédéric-Dupont, candidate of the *Giscardien* UDF and member of the RPR Parliamentary
Group. Gaullists and *Giscardiens* share the same electorate. In
social background and in opinions there is virtually no difference
between RPR and *Giscardien* supporters.[2] There is scarcely any

resistance by the electors of each to transfer their votes to the other at the second ballot[3]. The elites (and electors) of each formation share that strongest of all political adhesives anticommunism. In addition to their antipathy to Communists, the rival elites share a reluctance to let the opposition spoil the monopoly of influence, patronage, and power which the *majorité* in varying proportions has enjoyed for twenty years.

The irony in today's rivalry between Gaullists and *Giscardiens* is that there are far fewer deep-seated reasons for antagonisms than there were in the 1960's. When Giscard d'Estaing in 1967 criticised the 'solitary exercise of power' by General de Gaulle (in whose governments he had been quite content to serve) and promised only conditional support (*'oui, mais'*) he was taking his distance from those for whom Gaullism and the words and acts of the General were a kind of religion, a mystical and heroic epic.

The present leader of the Gaullist movement, Jacques Chirac, is not a 'heroic' Gaullist at all - he is a technocrat, a protégé of President Pompidou, and a pragmatist. Indeed, by backing Giscard d'Estaing and not Chaban-Delmas for the Presidency in 1974, and by taking the direction of the Gaullist Party away from the 'barons' of heroic Gaullism, he has done more to defeat historic Gaullism than anyone. Yet there is more apparent antagonism today between the *Chiraquiens* and the *Giscardiens* than ever before. It is territorial. The RPR wants the Presidency of the Republic back. It wants the Premiership back. It wants its dominance of the State, government, and Parliament, that it enjoyed in the Pompidou years back. Like a faction in Japanese politics, the RPR is the instrument of the ambition of Jacques Chirac and the hopes of patronage that would flow from his success.

In the weeks preceding the 1978 election antagonism within the *majorité* was, unlike within the left, fairly muted. The determination of the *Chiraquiens* to prevent the Prime Minister Raymond Barre appearing as anything like the official leader of the *majorité* and to ensure that the RPR remained the largest Parliamentary group continued nonetheless. Chirac's domination of the Gaullist Party began after the Presidential elections in 1974 when he was Prime Minister. He was able to turn the tables on those

who accused him of acting to defeat 'heroic Gaullism' by stating
his conviction, backed up by secret opinion polls to which as
Minister of the Interior he had had access, that Giscard d'Estaing
was the only person who could have beaten the 'Socialo-Communist'
candidate Mitterrand in the second ballot - a very plausible
argument. It was in 1974, when morale and opinion poll ratings
were at their lowest ebb, that Chirac made his famous promise to
Gaullist parliamentarians that he would lead them back, 150 strong,
at the next election. In December the same year, in a swifly exe-
cuted *coup*, he took control of the party by being elected Secretary-
General. In 1975 he was triumphantly received by a National Party
Congress at which his 'Gaullian style' was acclaimed. In 1976,
amidst growing rumours of disagreements with the President, he
resigned as Prime Minister. In October, in a speech at Egletons,
he announced that the party would be transformed into a *'vaste
rassemblement populaire'* and this was duly performed on December
5th before 50,000 people at the Porte de Versailles, under the
name RPR and with Chirac as President endowed with very wide powers
of personal direction. Since then there has been a continuous
period of attacks on the government and its policies accompanied
by protestations of loyalty to the *majorité* - the old *Giscardien*
tactic of *'oui, mais'*. Warfare between *Chiraquiens* and *Giscardiens* reached its most violent form during the Paris municipal
elections in March 1977. In July the components of the *majorité*
began a series of meetings to agree on election candidatures and
a manifesto. Servan-Schreiber, leader of the tiny Radical Party,
refused to attend and, more significantly, the Prime Minister was
not even invited. Chirac, having announced that the RPR would
present its own candidates and would fight the elections under its
own flag and not a united *majorité* banner, took badly the reve-
lation by Servan-Schreiber that the non-Gaullist elements of the
majorité were presenting a common front, a single set of candidates,
against the RPR. Despite this slightly bogus indignation and the
personal nature of all these rivalries, negotiations continued in
order to settle in which constituencies, for one reason or another,
RPR candidates or *Giscardien* candidates could be given an unopposed
clear run by the rest of the *majorité*. Chirac, himself, put his

energy to the unremitting task of campaigning throughout the country on behalf of RPR candidates - hoping thereby to establish himself as a recognised national leader, principal figure in the *majorité* and main adversary of Communism and the left, and to minimise the *Giscardien* challenge by getting his candidates through to the second ballot ahead of the *Giscardiens*.

It was perfectly clear to the non-RPR elements of the *majorité* that if each of them presented a candidate in a 'primary' with the RPR very few of them would succeed in becoming the sole candidate of the *majorité* in the second ballot. The meetings referred to by Servan-Schreiber, which were held in the Pavillon de Musique in the Prime Minister's garden, resulted in a list of candidates with the 'Presidential' investiture *Union pour la Démocratie Française* (UDF), a name chosen from the title of the little book of the thoughts of Giscard d'Estaing.[4] The UDF, which had quite a successful election and, as we shall see, succeeded in bringing to an end the long Gaullist dominance of the *majorité*, has persisted after the election - not yet as a French Liberal Party but at least as a Federation with an organisational structure and a staff. The UDF begins to fill an important vacuum in French politics - a big Presidential party. A President needs a party to give him political support and organisational backing in elections, in Parliament, and in other spheres. President Pompidou's immense authority was firmly based on the effectiveness of the Gaullist UDR. Equally, to be successful a party needs a Presidential figure it can identify with - the rise of the Gaullist Party during the Presidency of de Gaulle being the classic illustration. Thus the UDF was officially born on February 1st 1978 to combine during the election the efforts of the 'Presidential' and non-Gaullist components of the *majorité*.

c. Public opinion

In the months preceding the election, as Table 2.2 makes clear, opinion was remarkably stable. Every gain or loss of one percentage point was proclaimed with mighty headlines by the press, as if no-one had heard of the normal statistical margin of error

TABLE 2.2 Voting Intentions (Opinion Polls - A = SOFRES, B = IFOP)

	1974 June A	1976 Jan A	1976 Mar A	1976 June A	1976 Oct A	1977 May A	1977 June A	1977 Sept A	1977 Sept B	1977 Oct A	1977 Nov A	1977 Nov B	1977 Dec A	1978 Jan A	1978 Jan B	1978 Feb A	1978 Feb B	1978 Mar A	1978 Mar B	1978 Mar (11th)	Result 1st ballot (Mar 12th)
PCF	21	20	21	21	21	20	20	20	19	21	21	21	21	20	20	21½	21	21	21	20½	20.7
Ext. Left	3	3	2	2	3	3	3	2	3	2	2	4	2	2	2	2	2	2½	2	2	3.2
PS/MRG	27	30	30	28	28	30	30	31	28	27	26	26	27	30	28	29½	27	30	28	31	25.0
TOTAL LEFT	51	53	53	51	52	53	53	53	50	50	49	51	50	52	50	53	50	53½	51	53½	49.1
Ecologists & Others									5	3	4	4	3	4	6	3	5	3½	4	3½	4.8
Centrists	12	8	9	8	8	8	6	5	5	5	6		7								
UDF														20	20	20	19	20	20	18½	21.3
RI/PR	24	24	22	24	22	19	19	19	20	21	20	21	18								
RPR	13	15	16	17	18	20	22	23	20	21	21	24	22	21	22	21	22	20	22	21	22.5
Other *Maj.*														3	2	3	4	3	3	3½	2.0
TOTAL MAJORITE	49	47	47	49	48	47	47	47	45	47	47	45	47	44	44	44	45	43	45	43	45.9

Notes:
- Presidential Elections (May) — 1974
- Cantonal Elections (March) — 1976
- Formation of RPR (Dec 5) — 1976
- Municipal Elections (March) — 1977
- PS/PCF split (Sept 22) — 1977
- Speeches by Giscard d'Estaing / Verdun sur le Doubs - 27 Jan / Eve of poll, TV - 11 March — 1978

within which such changes fall. The principal characteristics to
emerge from this table are the the considerable and sustained lead
of Socialists over Communists, the strength of the *Giscardiens*
(RI/PR) in the period following the Presidential elections when
they received the full benefit of being considered the President's
party, and the gradual recovery of Gaullism from its low point
after the defeat of Chaban-Delmas in the Presidential elections.
There are three other comments to make when weighing the effectiveness of opinion polls as a guide to political opinion in France.
Firstly, the figure for those intending to vote Communist is an
estimate (based on long experience) rather than a finding. One
of the characteristics of many Communist electors is a reluctance
to declare their allegiance to public opinion polls. Secondly, as
we saw in the last chapter, there was a very significant gap between the proportion of electors declaring their intention to vote
for the left and the proportion who 'in their heart of hearts'
wanted the left to win. This-all important pointer to the even-
tual result is illustrated in Table 2.3. Note the big change in
hopes for a *majorité* victory in Autumn 1977 after the PS/PCF split
and when Communist aggressivity against the Socialists was at its
height.

TABLE 2.3   Overestimation of the Left

	June	Sept	1977 Oct	Nov	Dec	Jan	1978 Feb	Mar
Lead of left in opinion polls (voting intentions, SOFRES)	+6	+6	+3	+2	+3	+7	+7	+6
Lead of *majorité* in 'hopes to win'* (SOFRES)	-1	+3	+4	+10	+4	-1	+2	+2

* (*au fond de vous-même souhaitez-vous la victoire de . . .?*
   - 'in your heart of hearts, who do you hope will win?').

The third observation is that the division of choices within the *majorité* between RPR and UDF is modified if one replaces the name of the party with the names of the local candidates : 'do you intend to vote for Mr. X (UDF) or Mr. Y (RPR)?'. The answers to questions thus posed revealed the advantage to the RPR in having more well-known out-going deputies seeking re-election, and also the fact that preferences for one party or another within the *majorité* are not very strong.

Two final indications of the strength of rival political forces on the eve of the election deserve attention. The first is strength of the belief, as recorded in opinion polls, that the *majorité* were going to win - particularly after the crisis in the left in the Autumn of 1977 (Table 2.4).

TABLE 2.4   Public Predictions of Election Result

	June	Sept	1977 Oct	Nov	Dec	Jan	1978 Feb	Mar
Who do you think is going to win?								
Majorité	27	36	44	54	44	45	38	37
Left	47	32	26	18	23	25	34	31

The second and final indication is the rising popularity of President Giscard d'Estaing. In 1976 the proportion of people delcaring themselves satisfied with him dwindled from 57% to 39%, a record low for any President in the Fifth Republic. In the second half of 1977, however, things greatly improved. The Prime Minister, Raymond Barre, also reached his highest rating just before the elections, although in his case the number of dissatisfied continued slightly to outnumber the satisfied. There is very little in any of the poll findings about public opinion before the elections to indicate any very powerful mood of discontent.

TABLE 2.5   Popularity of Giscard d'Estaing and Barre
             (IFOP - *France Soir*)

	1977								1978		
	J	M	A	M	J	S	O	N	D	J	F
Giscard d'Estaing											
Satisfied %	41	45	43	40	48	49	51	51	52	55	56
Dissatisfied %	45	40	42	46	42	40	36	35	38	37	38
Barre											
Satisfied %	35	42	39	34	42	41	43	40	39	44	45
Dissatisfied %	44	42	45	50	45	46	43	45	49	46	48

NOTES

(1) See Jean-Luc Parodi 'L'union et la différence: les percep-
     tions de la gauche après la crise de septembre 1977' dans
     SOFRES L'opinion publique en 1977 Paris, Presses de la FNSP,
     1978.

(2) See R. Cayrol and J. Jaffré 'les électeurs de la majorité:
     unité et clivage' (le Monde, Dossiers et Documents, les
     élections législatives de mars 1978, pp. 56-7, and Ch. 5.

(3) See below Chapter 6, Table 6.7.

(4) Démocratie française, Paris, Fayard, 1976.

CHAPTER 3. CANDIDATES

Reference has already been made to the remarkable - indeed
record - number of candidatures for the 1978 elections. Table 3.1
shows the striking growth in the appeal of a parliamentary candidature:

Table 3.1 Candidatures - 5th Republic

	1958	1962	1967	1968	1973	1978
Candidates	3018	2228	2256	2314	3087	4268
No. per constituency	5.5	4.6	4.6	4.8	6.3	8.7

The reasons for this appeal are not very difficult to seek: the
opportunity for any organisation with at least 75 candidates to
address the nation free of charge on television, and the relatively low cost of a lost deposit (Frs 1000 plus the refund of some
printing expenses) if the threshold of 5% of the vote is not
attained. Another reason for the particularly high number of candidates in 1978 was, as we shall see, the lack of unity in almost
all camps. The *majorité* had multiple candidatures instead of one
official candidate per constituency. The left-Radicals contested
the Socialists in many constituencies where the two formations
normally present a united front. The Ecologists were divided into
rival factions as were the extreme left and the extreme right.
     Organisations presenting candidates include those in the
following list. If they had sufficient candidates (75) to quali-
fy for free television time, this fact is indicated:

                                          No. of candidates
                                          (metropolitan
                                          France)

Majorité

UDF *(Giscardiens: Union pour la Démocratie·*
     Français) (TV)   387

  - PR *(Parti Républicain)** (TV)

  - CDS *(Centre des Démocrates Sociaux)** (TV)

	No. of candidates (metropolitan France)
- Radical Party* (TV)	

CNIP *(Centre National des Indépendents et Paysans)*** (TV)

MDSF *(Mouvement Démocrate Socialiste de France)*** (TV)

*Démocratie Chrétienne*** (TV)

RPR (Gaullists: *Rassemblement pour la République)* (TV) — 401

   (* some candidates not endorsed by UDF)

   (** some candidates endorsed by UDF)

Left - *Programme Commun:-*

PS *(Parti Socialiste)* (TV)	442
MRG *(Mouvement des Radicaux de Gauche)* (TV)	121
PCF *(Parti Communiste Français)* (TV)	470

Extreme Left:-

- *Lutte Ouvrière* (TV) — 468

- *Ligue Communiste Revolutionnaire* (TV))
- *Organisation Communiste des*) — 187
  Travailleurs)

- *Front Autogestionnaire* (includes PSU - *Parti Socialiste Unifié*) (TV) — 221

- *Union ouvrière et paysanne pour la démocratie prolétarienne* (maoist) (TV)

Ecologists:- — 223

- *Ecologie – 78* (TV)

- *Paris – Ecologie*

Dissident Gaullists — 98

- UGP *(Union des Gaullistes de Progrès)*

- FRP *(Fédération des Républicains de Progrès)*

- UJP *(Union des Jeunes pour le Progrès)*

Extreme Right — 246

- *Parti des Forces Nouvelles* (TV)

- *Front National* (enough candidates for TV time but too late applying)

- *Nouvelle Action Française* (Royalists)

No. of candidates
(metropolitan
France)

Other Right   241

- *Union des Français de Bon Sens*

- *Action Republicaine Indépendente et
  Libérale* (TV)

- *Rassemblement des Usagers et
  Contribuables* (TV)

Other

- *Mouvement Démocrate (Jobertistes)* (TV)   89

- *Choisir* (Feminists)   43

- *Parti Socialiste Démocrate* (dissident
  Socialists)   66

There were also regionalist movements - Breton, Catalan,
Basque, Alsacian, Occitan, Corsican - who presented candidates,
the most important of which is *Union Démocratique Bretonne* (17 candidates). There were movements for the rights of homosexuals, for
civil rights for soldiers, and a multiplicity of other fragments
of the extreme left either anarchist or Trotskyist.

To this long (and incomplete) list are added innumerable
candidates who belong to no organisation, candidates who claim to
have no party affiliation (*sans étiquette*) but who in fact are
known to be official candidates of the *majorité*, and candidates
who are endorsed by more than one organisation - for instance like
the Prime Minister Raymond Barre. At least in 1978 the authori-
ties did not have to contend, as in 1973, with the 71 independent
candidates whose presence in two Corsican constituencies had the
sole purpose of frustrating the operation of the new fraud-proof
voting machines!

As far as the four main political tendencies are concerned
(UDF, RPR, PS/MRG, PC) the social characteristics of candidates
reveal some interesting differences (Table 3.2). As Table 3.2
shows the parties of the *majorité* - and the left-Radicals - draw
their candidates overwhelmingly from the social and economic élite,
the Socialists from the teaching profession and junior management.
The Communists have far more working-class candidates than anyone
else and their teacher candidates, though numerous, are more likely

TABLE 3.2 SOCIOLOGY OF CANDIDATES (MAIN PARTIES)

% of candidates for each party who are:-

	Average Age	Women	Top Civil Servants	ex-ENA	Employers	Liberal professions (med., law etc.)	High Income Sector	Junior Management	Teaching	Middle Sector	Clerical Workers	Manual Workers	Working Class	Farmers	Shopkeepers, artisans
RPR	48	2.7	7.2	3.9	26.5	23.3	59.3	16.3	9.7	26.0	2.8	0	2.8	3.8	1.9
PR	47	5.0	10.0	5.6	21.6	30.2	66.3	9.4	7.4	16.8	1.4	1.4	2.8	4.0	4.0
CDS	46	4.5	7.4	2.7	20.3	29.6	57.3	10.2	11.1	21.3	4.7	0	4.7	5.6	5.6
Rad	43	4.3	6.9	1.4	34.5	20.6	62.0	6.9	12.0	18.9	1.7	0	1.7	5.2	5.2
PS	43	5.1	5.2	4.3	10.7	11.3	33.7	15.1	38.7*	53.8	4.6	1.8	6.4	3.0	0.6
MRG	45	3.5	2.9	0.9	26.4	32.3	61.6	16.2	**	-	0	0	0	1.5	2.9
PCF	44	13.2	0	0	0.5	1.7	2.2	17.3	28.6*	45.9	11.3	32.3	43.6	2.2	1.3

* Of which Primary school 6.5% (PS) and 10.8% (PCF)

** figure not known

(Source: le Monde, 17 mars, 1978 - p. 13, Article by G. Fabre - Rosane and A. Guedé)

than the other parties to be drawn from the lower ranks of that
profession. The Communists are also the only party who can present anything like an honourable record in the selection of women
candidates - although 13.2% hardly reflects the proportion of
women in the population at large. Not surprisingly nearly all the
women in the National Assembly, 12 out of 19 to be precise, are
Communists. Though the *Giscardien* PR is the favoured party at the
moment of the French administrative élite, the Socialists were
able to present a number of ENA-trained top civil servants as candidates. As far as age is concerned, the greater average age of
majorité candidates reflects the high proportion of *députés* seeking re-election to be found in their ranks as well as their preference for selecting established local figures as candidates.
The Communists, as we shall see, have carried out a systematic renewal of their ageing parliamentarians.

Another important general characteristic of the election candidates for the principal parties is *implantation locale* - the pro-
pensity for them to be well-known local political figures like
councillors or mayors. Of course in most countries individuals
who become interested in political activity tend to serve on a
local council before they attain national elective office. However France presents some unusual characteristics. Influence in
national politics is very often based upon a political leader's
local influence. The influential role of Jacques Chaban-Delmas in
the Bordeaux area, of Jean Lecanuet in Rouen and Normandy, of
Gaston Defferre in Marseille, or of Jacques Chirac both in Paris
of which he is Mayor and in the Corrèze of whose *Conseil Général*
he is President, are all good examples. They are not merely, in
most cases, members of the National Assembly, or, on occasions
senior members of the government, they are also leading figures in
city and regional government. They can also claim to have an influence on public opinion, on voting, and, by lending or denying
their support, on the choice and success of candidates throughout
a whole region. Furthermore, although *parachutés* are quite often
successful candidates, there seems to be a built-in electoral advantage for the well-established local man and in some areas -

TABLE 3.3 *IMPLANTATION LOCALE* OF CANDIDATES
(main parties - metropolitan France)

A = No of candidates; B = % elected

	RPR A	RPR B	UDF A	UDF B	PS/MRG* A	PS/MRG* B	PCF A	PCF B	Total A	Total B
Députés sortants										
with local mandate(s)	101	86	79	80	74	79	46	89	300	83
without local mandate	26	73	18	61	5	80	12	83	61	72
Total	127	83	97	76	79	79	58	88	361	81
(% of constituencies**)	(27%)		(20%)		(17%)		(12%)		(76%)	
Mayor + *conseil général*	18	39	31	35	43	30	43	23	135	30
Mayor only	17	24	27	26	44	25	34	9	122	20
Conseil général and/or municipal council	34	24	40	28	85	20	90	16	249	20
Former *députés* (local), ex-mayors, Senators	15	13	4	25	-	-	3	-	22	14
Total 'notables'	211	60	199	52	251	41	228	34	889	46
('notables' as % of candidates)	(53%)		(52%)		(53%)		(48%)		(51%)	
('notables' as % of elected *députés*)	(90%)		(79%)		(93%)		(90%)		(87%)	

*   MRG candidates included only where no Socialist was standing

** *députés sortants* were re-elected in 62% of metropolitan constituencies

especially rural - a *parachuté* without local roots has very little
chance. The more local offices a candidate holds, the more his influence grows, and the greater his chances of success. 83% of all
députés sortants (members of Parliament seeking re-election) who
also had one or more local offices were re-elected, 72% of *députés
sortants* who had no local office, 30% of candidates who were mayors
and *Conseillers Généraux*, 20% of candidates who were either mayors
or local councillors. Altogether 87% of the assembly elected in
March 1978 were local notables of one sort or another (see
Table 3.3).

a. The *Majorité*

Passing from general characteristics of candidates we now
examine the tactical configuration. Where do the different parties
present candidates and where not? For the *majorité*, in particular,
what considerations determine whether a 'primary' election should
be held in a constituency? Should the public, that is to say, be
able to choose at the first ballot between different candidates
of the different parties of the *majorité* and determine by its votes
which candidate it prefers to be the sole standard-bearer in the
second decisive ballot? In 1967, when the *majorité* concept was
really launched for the first time under the leadership of Prime
Minister Georges Pompidou, there were no officially encouraged primaries. Pompidou declared, at the outset of the negotiations
between Gaullists and *Giscardiens* over the designation of official
'Fifth Republic' candidates in each constituency: 'a candidate will
be adopted by the *majorité* in every constituency. There will be
only one candidate adopted in each constituency. That there will be
dissidents is possible, even probable. But they will be known as
dissidents and the electors will be informed.'[1] This iron-disci-
pline relaxed as the years passed. There were 50 first ballot
'primaries' between rival candidates of the *majorité* in 1968, and
61 in 1973. In 3 cases in 1973 Gaullist deputies seeking re-
election were actually defeated by *Giscardiens*.[2]

In 1978, with a *majorité* that since the Presidential election
of 1974 had included all the old opposition centre, it was decided
to encourage 'pluralism' - 'primaries' virtually everywhere.
Gaullists and *Giscardiens* all wanted the maximum opportunity to
become the leading element of the *majorité*. As recounted in the
last chapter, however, and to the chagrin of Jacques Chirac, the
non-RPR parties of the *majorité* decided to agree amongst themselves
not to present more than one non-RPR candidate in any constituency.
There were therefore two sets of negotiations going on. One in
the Pavillon de Musique in the garden of the Prime Minister's
official residence involved the *Giscardiens* and centrists - later
to become jointly the UDF - on who in each constituency should be
the sole standard-bearer of the UDF. The second set of negotiations involving both *Giscardiens* and the RPR, sorted out which
constituencies should have 'primaries' and which should be
'reserved' for a single candidate. Primaries were not held in
130 out of the 474 constituencies of metropolitan France (27%).
Ministers in almost all cases were allowed a clear run - it would
have looked bad if members of the government were eliminated by
government supporters. Very solidly entrenched *députés* seeking
re-election often had a clear run merely because it was pointless
to attempt to dent their majorities. Often they were prominent
political and party leaders like Chirac, Chaban-Delmas, or Edgar
Faure or prestigious figures, locally and nationally, like Marcel
Dassault or the Mayor of Toulouse Pierre Baudis, so that prudence
and deference joined forces with calculation. In a number of
opposition strongholds there was only one candidate of the *majorité*
because the other parties were too weak in that locality to produce a candidate. An important aspect of party organisation within the *majorité* is 'prospecting' for suitable candidates, and in
some places, in the Socialist South-West for instance, the search
was obviously unsuccessful. In some cases, Audinot in Somme 5,
Hunault in Loire-Atlantique 4, or Hersant, the newspaper tycoon,
in Hauts-de-Seine 6, for example, candidates under the guise of
independence were endorsed by both wings of the *majorité* or at
least opposed by neither. There were a number of deals: it appears,

for instance, that Alain Griotteray, negotiating for a time on behalf of the PR, was willing to make a lot of concessions to the RPR in return for a clear run in the constituency (Paris 21) he had chosen for a parliamentary come-back.[3] In a number of marginal constituencies, finally, a *député sortant*, obviously facing a difficult battle because his constituency had voted for Mitterrand in 1974, was allowed to devote himself to the main task of keeping the Socialists and Communists out. Examples include Boinvilliers (RPR - Cher 2) or Commenay (UDF - Landes 3).

As will already be clear from the preceding paragraph, candidate selection within the *majorité* is carried out by party leaderships. Consultation with local people is a part of the process but there is no local selection conference as in a British political party or the French Socialist Party. The preparative work for the RPR was carried out under the direction of M. Toubon at party headquarters. 'Prospecting' began over 2 years before the election. Toubon toured the country visiting local political élites and, 'naturally' (so we were informed), consulting the *Préfets* and *Sous-préfets*, the senior government officials in the regions, on the suitability of potential candidates. When the RPR had a suitable candidate, endorsement was decided, where it had not, and where a *parachuté* was not likely to succeed, the RPR was prepared to do a deal and support a candidate of one of their partners in the *majorité*. Toubon did not himself handle the negotiations with partners but the results of his efforts were before those like Yves Guéna and Charles Pasqua who did. The principal objectives for the RPR leadership was the return of 150 *députés* to the new Assembly. This largely meant relying on locally well-entrenched members seeking re-election - protected where practicable or desirable from challenge at a 'primary'. In some RPR seats new candidates were designated. Sometimes death or voluntary retirement left a vacancy - as in the case of Oise 5 now occupied by a *Chiraquien* ENA graduate, J-F Nancel. Sometimes sitting members were forced out and replaced. Hoffer, for instance, the *député* for Epinal (Vosges 1) was replaced by another ENA *Chiraquien* from the Prime Minister's *cabinet* Philippe Séguin. The RPR presented 401 candidates for the 474 metropolitan constituencies.

TABLE 3.4 <u>UDF Candidates</u> (Metropolitan France)

	Total candidates		Eliminated in 1st ballot		Defeated at 2nd Ballot		Winners	
	No.	(% of UDF)	No.	(% of party)	No.	(% of party)	No.	(% of party)
PR	194	(50)	87	(45)	41	(21)	66	(34)
CDS	98	(25)	46	(47)	21	(21)	31	(32)
Rad	56	(14)	40	(71)	8	(14)	8	(14)
CNI	13	(3)	3		4		6	
MDSF	6	(2)	4		1		1	
DC*	3	(1)	1		1		1	
Maj.+	17	(4)	4	(23)	3	(18)	10	(59)
	387	(100)	185	(48)	79	(20)	123	(32)

* Christian Democrats

+ unspecified party affiliation

TABLE 3.5 PCF renewal: (Communist seat - C; Winnable seat - W)

André Lajoinie, 45, editor of <u>la Terre</u> (PCF agricultural weekly), *Bureau politique*	Allier 3 (C)
Guy Hermier, 37, *Agrégé*, Central Committee	Bouches-du-Rhône 4 (C)
Jeanine Porte, 44, Central Committee	Bouches-du-Rhône 7 (C)
Alàin Bocquet, 31, Central Committee	Nord 19 (W)
Maxime Gremetz, 37, *Bureau politique*	Somme 1 (C)
Paulette Fost, 39, Central Committee	Seine St Denis 1 (C)
Pierre Zarka, 29, Asst. General Secretary of *Jeunesse Communiste*	Seine St Denis 2 (C)
Charles Fiterman, 43, *Bureau politique*, Secretary of Central Committee	Val de Marne 2 (C)

The problem for the parties that united to form the UDF was to conduct negotiations with the RPR in such a way as to give a real chance for increased parliamentary representation, to find suitable candidates for designation, but, above all in the early stages, to agree amongst themselves so as not to duplicate their candidatures. The Pavillon de Musique negotiations between the partners eventually led to an agreed list of UDF candidates published in an official booklet. Agreement was not totally achieved on single candidatures: in 13 constituencies 2 UDF candidates were designated. In another 10 where a UDF candidate was officially adopted, individual parties from the UDF supported their own candidates and two of them were eventually elected. In total, 387 official UDF candidates contested 374 metropolitan constituencies. Thus 100 constituencies were left for the RPR alone - not counting isolated cases such as the ex-President of the Assembly Edgar Faure, adopted as UDF, in reality RPR, and acknowledging neither. Table 3.4 gives the breakdown of UDF candidates and their respective fates.

Half of all UDF candidates came from the Republican Party. About a third of PR, CDS, and indeed of all UDF candidates were elected. Those who were endorsed by the UDF but accepted no specified party label were often very strong and well-known figures like the Prime Minister Raymond Barre - and this explains their high rate of success. Of some significance is the failure of the Radicals who, like their *frères ennemis* the MRG, had too little popular appeal to benefit from their place in alliance with important parties.

b. The Left

On the left the picture is considerably simpler. The PCF by tradition has a candidate in every constituency - so 'primaries' within the left are universal. The non-Communist parties of the *union de la gauche*, like the non-Gaullist parties of the *majorité*, agree amongst themselves on a single candidate for each constituency. Socialists and Radicals fought the 1967 and 1968 elections under the joint label FGDS (Federation of the Democratic and Socialist Left). Socialists and MRG in 1973 combined together to

call themselves UGSD (Union of the Socialist and Democratic Left).
The same general pattern applied in 1978 though there were some
differences. Firstly, there were 4 constituencies without a
Communist candidate. In Val d'Oise 1 and Alpes-Maritimes 2, the
PCF supported dissident Gaullists against the well-known pro-
government figures of Poniatowski and Jacques Médecin respectively.
In Rhône 6 and Yvelines 4 the PCF supported PSU candidates.
Secondly, the Socialists and MRG decided in two constituencies to
lend their support to Independents rather than present candidates
of their own. One was the controversial Mayor of Cannes Cornut-
Gentille, the other de Chambrun in Lozère 2. Finally there were
some 'primaries' between PS and MRG. In 31 constituencies out of
474 in metropolitan France, the MRG was allowed a clear run with
no Socialist rival. In the remainder there were a number of MRG
candidates but, except in a handful of cases, they made no impact
whatsoever, and troubled the Socialists not at all. Sometimes,
the few votes that they collected were of great importance, and it
seems, the PCF encouraged and even lent resources to these minor
MRG candidates. For instance in Essonne 4, the Socialist Yves
Tavernier would have eliminated a Communist *député* seeking re-
election but for the 1200 votes that went to the MRG candidate.

In the selection of candidates, local sections in the
Communist Party are closely consulted, and the Party decides on
the basis of recommendations by the Federations (*Département*
level) to the Central Committee. The operation is carefully
planned over several years. If a well-known Communist member of
Parliament is nearing retirement, his designated replacement is
given every opportunity to become well-known by acquiring local
office as Mayor or Councillor. There were a number of examples in
1978 of young and leading members of the Party being planted in
safe Communist seats (see Table 3.5).

The Socialist Party is the most 'British' of French political parties in the sense that it is the party membership in the
constituencies, subject to certain constraints and to ratification
by party headquarters, that makes the choice. Nearly all outgoing members were re-selected but a number of leading party figures like Michel Rocard (Yvelines 3, elected), Lionel Jospin

(Paris 26 - defeated), Georges Sarre (Paris 10 - defeated), or Bernard Derosier (Nord 4 - elected) were selected in what looked like winnable seats. Other members of the party leadership were selected in strong left-wing constituencies held by the Communists! Michel Charzat (Paris 30), Yves Tavernier (Essonne 4), and Pierre Bérégovoy (Nord 22), for example, greatly annoyed the PCF by attempting to poach on their territory - and, in more than one case, very nearly succeeding.

One of the main themes of any study of the 1978 elections in France is the rivalry and defensiveness that prevailed within both big alliances. This is seen at its clearest at the level of candidatures.

NOTES

(1) Centre d'étude de la vie politique française Les élections législatives de mars 1967, Paris, Cahiers de la FNSP 170, 1971, p. 23.

(2) Lozère 2, Ain 3, Rhône 8.

(3) In the end he did not get even the UDF endorsement in Paris 21 and was defeated by Gantier who did.

CHAPTER 4. THE CAMPAIGN

a. Local and National Campaigning

The campaign for the 1978 election, having really begun
after the Presidential Election of 1974, was exceedingly long. A
single issue predominated and earned the campaign the attention
of the whole world: communist participation in goverment if the
left won. Because it was so long and because one issue loomed so
large, it was an election campaign of extreme banality. At national level there was hardly any discussion of foreign affairs,
of defense, or energy problems, nor even, from government supporters, a serious presentation of the Fifth Republic's really quite
creditable record over twenty years of national renewal, social
progress, and economic achievement. However, as usual in French
democracy, there is a profound distinction to be drawn between
the campaign at national level and the campaigns at local level.
In this respect French politics resembles American and differs
sharply from British politics. In Great Britain there is virtually
no local dimension to a national election campaign. A local issue,
a well-established local parliamentarian, the support of a well-
known local figure - these things count for virtually nothing.
Even in local elections, local issues are of marginal importance.
Even the phenomena of Welsh or Scottish nationalism are best under-
stood primarily as protests against national government and its
two great parties. In the United States the local standing of a
candidate and his position on local issues is important. In
France, despite the 'nationalisation' of politics through television, local aspects of a national election are significant,
though it would be difficult to quantify them as a variable in
the outcome. One numerical indicator can be found by comparing
constituency by constituency the score of the left at the first
ballot in 1978 with the percentage obtained by Mitterrand at the
2nd ballot of the Presidential election in 1974 (Table 4.1).
Nationally both totals were roughly equal at around 49%. However
in constituencies where there was a *député* of the left seeking
re-election, the left did even better than Mitterrand in two-thirds

45

of cases - this figure being almost the same where the *sortant* was communist or socialist. In constituencies where the *député* seeking re-election was from the *majorité*, the left, by contrast, declined in two-thirds of cases.

TABLE 4.1 <u>ABOVE AVERAGE PERFORMANCE OF *DEPUTES SORTANTS*</u>

Gain or decline of left from 1974 (Mitterrand - 2nd ballot) to 1978 (1st ballot) (Metropolitan)

	Left gain	Left no change or loss
Constituencies with:		
Député sortant - *majorité* (224)	33%	67%
Député sortant - left (135*)	64%	36%
- PS/MRG (77*)	(66%)	(34%)
- PCF (58)	(61%)	(39%)

(* not counting Corsica - constituencies affected by boundary changes)

There are other indicators of the impact of local issues and local personalities. The best results obtained by the Ecologists, for example, were in areas where nuclear reactors were being built. In the 3 constituencies round the nuclear reprocessing plants and reactors near Cherbourg, the Ecologists obtained 8, 10 and 13% of first ballot votes. The extreme left obtained its best score in the constituency where its best-known personality Arlette Laguiller was a candidate.

In France it is at local level that one finds the authentic expression of both the popular sagacity and narrow-minded egoism that are the two sides of democracy in any country. The local activities of candidates and party workers consist largely in the publication and distribution of statements and leaflets, sticking posters, and holding meetings in every town or village. Each candidate makes an official address to the electors in two forms - a poster which appears on official sites outside town halls and polling stations and a single sheet leaflet which is circulated,

along with the declarations of all other candidates, in a mailing
carried out by and at the cost of the local prefecture. This is
a most valuable and democratic practice - it means that every
elector receives all information in one envelope about all the
candidates and their platforms. It means that party workers do
not have to waste their time, as in Great Britain, writing out
addresses, and that candidates who have no party workers are still
able to communicate to their electors. The official envelope
mailed to all electors before the first ballot in Nord 3 (Lille)
yields the following interesting messages:

RPR *député* seeking re-election: (blue type, glossy paper) -
> stresses the positive record of the government,
> the danger of chaos if the left is elected, the
> support of Raymond Barre. No mention of de Gaulle.

UDF: messages from Giscard d'Estaing and Raymond Barre.
> A vote for Vouters is a vote for Giscard.

Socialist candidate - a woman - close print, argumentative,
boring and unreadable.
> Socialists will increase purchasing power in order
> to end economic crisis.

Communist candidate - well-produced, two colours, photos,
simple messages.
> Vote Communist in order to live better. For real
> change vote Communist: Communist ministers (bold type)
> in a government of the left.

MRG: the left that is reasonable and sensible.

Mouvement Démocrate (Jobertistes): end division of the
country into two blocs.

OCT (*Organisation Communiste des Travailleurs*):
> Not enough to change government, change society.
> No confidence in PS or PCF but better to vote for
> them in the second ballot.

If there is a second ballot the electors all receive a second
mailing in which the candidates that remain make new declarations
and indicate the support they have from first ballot candidates
who have now withdrawn in their favour. Sometimes, especially in
those rare cases where all the left has been eliminated and the
two candidates in the second ballot both belong to the *majorité*,
the declarations become quite personal. For instance the UDF

candidate in Paris 4 said at the second ballot: 'the *député sortant* (RPR) embodies dreary, authoritarian, and rigid conservatism'. Appealing desperately to Socialist and Communist electors with no candidate of their own to support, he added in bold type 'to abstain is to vote for Pierre Bas'. His rival in his declaration replies 'don't take the risk of electing a man who will be dependent upon . . . the parties of the left and even the extreme-left'. Election leaflets (first and second) ballot have interesting details too. The *suppléant*, who would take over as parliamentary representative if the *député* dies or becomes a minister, figures almost as prominently as the candidate on the leaflets, and indeed in the campaign as a whole - a valuable apprenticeship process. If a candidate has a large number of children, that fact never fails to appear on an election leaflet because it informs Catholic electors that the candidate is one of them.

Other activities involving the printed word include sticking posters everywhere - nocturnally and illegally for the most part. Rival poster-sticking gangs sometimes encounter one another at dead of night and fights ensue. The result of this intense activity is that for years afterwards almost every wall or telegraph pole in France bears a souvenir of the campaign. As well as posters, the parties produce tracts and newspapers - on quite a large scale sometimes. The Socialist Party in the Nord for example has its own printing works. There are brochures on policy, leaflets on local issues, denunciations of rival candidates (who refuse a public debate for example), announcements of meetings, special numbers of new-born local newspapers like le Travailleur Vosgien, and explanations as to how François Mitterrand, or the President of the Republic, or the Prime Minister wishes the recipient to vote.

Meetings play an important part in a French election campaign. They are of two types. There is the large, well-attended, widely-reported meeting held in the constituency's largest town. Local figures, like mayors or senators, will speak on behalf of the candidate and his *suppléant*. The attendance will be larger and the impact greater if a national leader like Marchais or Chirac speaks - but the main campaign meeting is well-attended and will have wide coverage in the local press - and France, let us not forget, is a country of local newspapers. In la Presse de la Manche for instance, on March 7th, the visit of Raymond Barre was the lead, with a very large photo, on page 1 and the whole of page 2, while other election news covers a further 2½ pages - all in an 18 page local paper. The larger meetings are very useful for resounding declarations by candidates on local issues. The Liberté de l'Est of March 9th, for instance, carried a prominent story of an election meeting where the local RPR candidate undertook to save the jobs of a textile factory threatened by the Boussac bankruptcy. His campaign consisted largely of hinting that his influence in high places (he was in Raymond Barre's *cabinet*) would be directed towards obtaining favours for his constituency, so he made a 'solemn engagement' to save the threatened jobs, and to resign within a year if he had not succeeded. He did not need to resign. A new 'plan for the Vosges' was announced in August 1978.

The other type of meeting - really fascinating to the foreign observer - is the small meeting held systematically in every village where the candidate meets the Mayor, his principal council colleagues, and any members of the public who are able to come. The mayor of a small rural village is regarded as having a great deal of influence over the way his villagers vote and one can see, at these meetings in the *salle des fêtes* at the *Mairie*, with the bags of rat-poison or agricultural leaflets stacked along the wall, the candidates being weighed up with a good deal of non-ideological peasant shrewdness. The capacity of a candidate to handle such a meeting with authority and attentiveness is a real mark of his calibre and, in a marginal constituency, very often an indication as to whether he really has the weight for the distance. In urban areas one encounters another type of small local meeting: the *permanence*. Where a *député* is seeking re-election, a favourite device he employs is to demonstrate how much more influence he has than other candidates. A leaflet will be distributed to all households indicating that he will be available to constituents at the Café du Commerce at a certain time. The candidate arrives without ceremony. There are a few perfunctory handshakes. There is no speech and the majority of drinkers

remain undisturbed. In a room at the back, however, the candidate's clientele is waiting: a line of people with minor individual problems like difficulty over a pension or the installation
of a telephone, or a relative wanting a job in the public service.
In other words it is roughly what a British MP calls his constituency 'surgery' - except that in Great Britain 'surgeries' are
not a feature of election campaigns.

On the national level there were the ceaseless activities of
what Michel Jobert cleverly named the 'gang of four' - Barre,
Mitterrand, Marchais and Chirac - and there was television which
presented very little other than the activities of the gang of
four. National campaign activity falls into two categories: the
official television and radio campaign and the day to day campaign activities (meetings and political statements of party
leaders).

Television, in a survey carried out by Louis Harris (France)
in February 1978, unsurprisingly comes out top as the preferred
medium of political information. In response to the question
'which, from this list, do you personally find the most useful
in helping you to know who to vote for?', 58% mentioned television, 41% newspapers, 28% radio, and 22% conversations. Meetings,
leaflets, posters, and opinion polls were nowhere near these
levels. In addition 66% of people thought television informed
them fairly well or very well, against only 19% with a bad opinion. 48% of respondents considered television to be politically
unbiassed. 34% (especially younger voters and supporters of the
left) considered that television favoured the government, 3% that
it favoured the left. The most-favoured type of political programme, according to the survey, is the debate between two leaders -
the fashion begun by Nixon and Kennedy in America in 1960 which
finally came to France in the 1974 Presidential election with the
big debates between Mitterrand and Giscard d'Estaing. This type
of television heavyweight championship was not used during the
1978 campaign. Absent too, from television though not from radio,
was the programme in which a single election issue - like education or economic policy - is discussed in depth.

The official campaign on television allows equal segments
of time for the *majorité* and the opposition with additional segments for 'organisations not represented in the National Assembly'
provided that they present at least 75 candidates at the first
ballot. All 11 of the latter, from the *Ligue Communiste Révolu-
tionnaire* to the extreme right-wing *Forces Nouvelles* have seven
minutes before the first ballot and another 5 before the second -
even though all of them (except for organisations like CNIP and
Christian Democracy who had candidates endorsed by the *majorité*)
had had all their candidates eliminated. In the segments for the
majorité and the opposition time was split by negotiation - on
the approximate basis of parliamentary strength in the old
Assembly. The RPR had the greatest exposure and the *majorité*
contrived to divide its time in such a way as to have 2 more
broadcasts than the opposition.

TABLE 4.2 Official Television Campaign

RPR	12 broadcasts	81 minutes
UDF	10	54
(PR)	(5)	(26)
(CDS/Rad)	(3)	(19)
(UDF)	(2)	(9)
Majorité	22	135
PS	10	69
PCF	9	57
MRG	1	9
Opposition	20	135

In the week before the second ballot the *majorité* received the
considerable bonus of spine-chilling anti-Communist homilies to
the nation by most of the fringe organisations who advised their
supporters to join forces with the *majorité* to save the country
from the totalitarian jackboot. The opposition had the dubious
advantage of television endorsement by the Trotskyist and anarchist organisations - an endorsement which usually consisted of
the assertion that it did not matter who won the elections, that
the Socialists and Communists were just as rotten as the capitalist parties, but that, rather than stay at home, revolutionaries
were on the whole advised to go and vote for the left.

The official campaign is presented in a singularly boring manner. There are no films in the manner of American politics or of the British Conservative Party's television 'commercials'. There are merely talking heads in a studio - sometimes alone, sometimes not, sometimes being 'interviewed'. Usually the leading party figures were presented - with the occasional young candidate getting a chance. The themes were predictable: anti-communism from the *majorité* and the right, emphasis on the misery and injustice which they would change from the Communists, and attempt to recapture the style of lyrical exultation that had sustained them for several years from the Socialists. The UDF saved for their last broadcast the Prime Minister Raymond Barre and for the first and last the woman health minister (not a candidate) who had proved to be the most popular government member at all times since the Presidential election, Simone Veil. Occasionally an ostensibly non-political figure arrested the attention. Jacques Cousteau, for instance, the famous underwater explorer represented the Ecologists in a passionate broadcast in which he said how intolerable the Mediterranean was for divers.

The official campaign appeared on all three TV channels from 8.30 to 9 o'clock every evening. In the Harris survey already quoted, 29% of people claimed to have watched all or nearly all of them, 8% to have watched only their own party's, 38% a few broadcasts here and there, and 19% none or hardly any. This dedication falls perhaps into perspective when one considers replies to the next question: did respondents think that all three channels should carry the election programmes or just one so that viewers could watch something else? 81% would have liked the opportunity to switch over.

The four main political leaders - Barre, Mitterrand, Marchais, and Chirac - toured the country addressing large meetings. The largest by far was the huge RPR rally addressed by Jacques Chirac at the Porte de Pantin in Paris on February 11th, where there were 100,000 people. The main function of these meetings is to demonstrate massive support and provide material for television and newspaper coverage. The threat of communism predominated as the theme that received coverage. This was not only because that was the principal theme projected by Chirac and

others but because the conflict between the parties of the left,
the singularly aggressive tone of the Communists and their ever-more
extreme demands for radical change, made the Communists the pivot
of the electoral campaign. For instance, insofar as economic
policy was an electoral issue it centred around the quarrels over
the minimum wage and over nationalisation. The Communists had
raised the bidding early in the history of their conflict with
the Socialists by demanding an immediate increase in the minimum
wage of about 37% to Fr 2400 a month. The Socialists, whose
initial reaction was that so large and sudden an increase would
be inflationary, eventually agreed to the figure. During this
debate the PCF repeatedly charged its partner of not really car-
ing about the underprivileged. After agreement was reached the
Socialists were an easy target for the *majorité*: charged with
eccnomic irresponsibility and giving way to the Communists every
time. It was the same with nationalisation: the less the Socialists agreed to, the more they were attacked by the PCF; the more
they agreed to the more they were attacked by everyone else.
The economic danger to the country of a left-wing government so
constituted and so divided was, as we shall see, the main theme
of President Giscard d'Estaing in his two speeches. Another
example of how the PCF made itself the pivot of the campaign was
over the issue of Communist participation in government. 'Yes,
there will be Communist ministers' was the bold PCF poster! The
Party would demand a full role in government and it would not
be a government that would 'manage the crisis' for capitalism
but a government that would fundamentally change the economy and
society; conditions would immediately improve for workers, in
terms of wages, holidays, and social benefits, and 'we will make
the rich pay' - a phrase repeated over and over with aggressive
relish. Thus all the anti-Communist election themes of the
majorité received from the PCF all the endorsement they needed.
It was easy for the press to present the agreement between Socialists and Communists for the second ballot over 'a proportional
distribution' of ministries in a government of the left as
'Mitterrand has yielded to the Diktat of Marchais' (Figaro,
page 1, headline, 15 March 1978) when Marchais himself eagerly
agreed that Communists would insist on top portfolios like Defence
or Foreign Affairs.

b. Finance

   All the main parties seemed to be extremely well-financed
and extremely reticent about the true cost of their campaigns,
which are becoming increasingly elaborate and expensive in France.
Donations from activists and sympathisers and the contribution
from the taxpayer in the form of certain legally reimbursed campaign expenses (election address and material mailed to each
elector, for example - see Chapter 3 - amounting in 1973 to
Fr 73 million) cannot possibly meet the entire cost. Travel for
ministers and party leaders, the cost of organising meetings with
stewards and a *service d'ordre*, posters on commercial prime sites,
special opinion polls and attitude surveys, books, stickers,
tee-shirts, books of matches, leaflets, newspapers, press-
receptions - these are vastly expensive items. The huge RPR meeting at Porte de Pantin, for instance, cost Frs 12 million according to the Canard Enchainé and the RPR's series of nationalistic
posters showing French exploits like Concorde is estimated to
have cost Frs 2 million plus production costs. Yet the RPR
claims to have spent only Frs 10 million for the entire campaign.
   A well-researched article in le Monde[1] hints at other
sources - public funds and industrial contributions. Public funds,
it is suggested, are employed in a variety of forms from the use
of municipal printing resources to the promotion of *majorité* candidates by advertising agencies who have been entrusted with
official public-service advertising for road safety, army recruit-
ment, the postal services and so on. Members of *cabinets*, ministerial and municipal staff, parliamentary assistants - innumerable public employees are detached for party work during and outside election campaigns. There was, in addition, the allegation
that UDF candidates were receiving subsidies from the Prime
Minister's official budget (heading: 'miscellaneous expenditure') -
an allegation rejected by Raymond Barre (le Monde 27-28 February)
in the form of a statement that such a suggestion was unworthy.
There is the familiar allegation that Communist municipalities
arrange for commissions to be paid to firms close to the Party
on municipal contracts for items like school furniture. There
are the activities of front organisations like the Association

for Democracy directed by Michel Bassi, a former Presidential
spokesman, which, according to le Monde, claims a monthly budget
of only Frs 100,000 contributed by members and donors, and yet
employs 40 staff, issues a large number of publications, and or-
ganises campaign meetings for ministers. Finally there is the
very large and virtually uncharted area of industrial donations
to all the non-Communist parties but particularly, of course, to
the *majorité*. Sometimes these are direct and well-known - as in
the case of the large contributions by Marcel Dassault to the RPR
generally and to his own campaign in the Oise where he makes gen-
erous and fairly public donations to municipalities in his constituency for the construction of public amenities. Little, however, is known about contributions made by large firms in the private sector, or industry associations, or employers' federations.
Since the election President Giscard d'Estaing has proposed a
system of direct subsidies to political parties along the lines
of what is done in West Germany. This would undoubtedly go some
way to clean up what, in all democracies, tends to be a rather
murky area - but the idea has already encountered strong opposition from the RPR. *A suivre.*

c. Party policies and subsidiary issues

       In an election everyone has a programme but some are even
less important than others. The significance of the famous
Programme commun of the left consisted less in its rather vague
content ('a gigantic improvisation' Raymond Barre called it) than
in its symbolic value as a historic compromise between Socialists
and Communists, a rallying point, and, ultimately, the pretext
for division and conflict. On the right election programmes are
traditionally less important and the main interest was whether
there would be one at all. Jacques Chirac refused to subscribe
to anything that could be called a 'programme of the *majorité*'
though the RPR issued its own proposals on traditional Gaullist
themes like national independence, profit-sharing with workers,
and economic policies favouring growth and an attack on unemployment. Finally the Prime Minister Raymond Barre took the initiative by issuing in a speech at Blois on January 7th 1978 a list

of 30 objectives and 110 proposals which would constitute a programme of action for the next five years. The *'programme de
Blois'* in this respect resembled the *'programme de Provins'* which
Messmer, the Gaullist Prime Minister in 1973, had issued before
the previous election. The programme included, in addition to
promises on economic development, improved pensions, or measures
to favour home-ownership, an interesting section on the rights of
the citizen which has the true Giscardian flavour. A kind of
Habeas Corpus would be introduced against arbitrary detention;
there would be new rules concerning interrogation by the police;
there would be clearer explanations from the administration about
decisions taken, rights of appeal, and reparation; there would be
an ombudsman (*médiateur*) in every *département*; there would be
more local control over local decisions and local taxation and
even local referenda at the initiative of council or citizens.
These proposals are sufficiently important, modest, and precise
to make one feel hopeful that the President will see them through
to implementation.

The older and more celebrated rival to the *Programme de
Blois*, the left's *Programme Commun*, was signed in 1972 and had
four main parts: change to a better life, democracy at work, democratic institutions, and contributing to peace. The first part
included promises for altered priorities in favour of the underprivileged in incomes, employment, health, social security, hous-
ing, transport, education and so on. The section entitled *'démo-
cratiser l'entreprise'* contained many seeds of future conflict
between the signatory parties. A lot of it reflects the ideas on
workers' control (*autogestion*) which are active in the Socialist
Party: workers' control of hiring and firing, accounts to be open
to workers, extended rights for unions and, finally, the right of
workers in a firm to demand its nationalisation. Communists were
never totally at their ease with the utopian and libertarian concept of *autogestion*. The section also contains the precise list
of companies and industries to be nationalised - a list whose re-
vision provoked the break-up of the *Union de la Gauche* in September
1977. Under institutions, Habeas Corpus, a supreme constitutional
court, and the suppression of counter-espionage and counter-subver-
sion police forces would improve liberties. Plurality of parties

would be guaranteed, and the signatory parties undertook to withdraw from power if they lost the confidence of the country. The
powers of the President of the Republic, notably to govern alone
in an emergency and to hold referenda, would be limited. Parliament would have greater powers. The incoming government would
give precise undertakings to the country in the form of a *con-
trat de législature*. *'Pantouflage'*, the practice of private
sector firms recruiting top civil servants, would be suppressed.
Government interference in television and radio would end. In
foreign affairs and defence (*'contribuer à la paix'*) the left
would scrap the French nuclear deterrent, would pursue, within
existing alliances, a policy independent of both military blocs,
would seek to create a less capitalist EEC and would recognise
the right to self-determination of French territories overseas.

The prolonged attempt to 'up-date' the *Programme Commun*
which was the pretext for such bitter and suicidal conflict in
the summer of 1977 covered the whole range of policies, which had
after all been drawn up five years earlier. The main points of
discord in the 'better life' section was the figure for the minimum wage and whether, to reduce inequality, the national spread
of incomes between the highest and lowest paid should be reduced
to 7 to 1 (PS) or 5 to 1 (PCF). Although inequality is a major
grievance in France and an important electoral issue, the fruit-
less conflict over exact figures between Socialists and Communists in a field where exactitude is impossible did a great deal
to undermine the credibility of a government of the left. Under
democracy at work the main bone of contention was an equally tri-
vial debate about extending nationalisation, and whether companies in which nationalised companies held shares should be nationalised too. There was also division over *autogestion:* both parties wanted the workers to elect at least one-third of the board
of directors but the Communists wanted the elections to be on
the basis of lists presented by the Unions. On defence there
was another major dispute. The PCF suddenly decided that the
maintenance of the nuclear deterrent was a good thing as was the
old Gaullist nationalist posture of defence *'tous azimuts'* - 'all
points of the compass' (i.e. against invasion by America or

Great Britain as well as by the Soviet Union). The PS agreed
provisionally to the maintenance of the nuclear *force de frappe*
and proposed, to the horror of the PCF, a referendum to decide
the issue. Whether the disputes were papered over or left unres-
olved, whether they concerned a vital issue or an unimportant one,
the credibility of the left never recovered from these debates.

Naturally the electorate at large did not read the fine
print of either the *Programme de Blois* or the *Programme Commun*
(authorised or revised version). However adversaries or interest groups raised the issues they considered relevant. The questions of nationalisation and workers' control were raised with
great concern by the business community. When the left broke up
in disagreement on 23rd September 1977, the Stock Exchange, seeing, as a spokesman put it, 'the totalitarian spectre moving away',
had a memorable day. Other interest groups drew electors' attention to other matters. One issue that had quite an impact was
that of the private (mainly Catholic) sector of education.
Catholic-centred interest groups reacted badly to the proposal
by the left that schools receiving public funds should be inte-
grated into the public education system. Why the left chose to
re-awaken this all but dead issue is a mystery. The conflict
over religious and secular education was a dominant issue in the
old days of republicans against monarchists and clericals against
anti-clericals. The left, by raising that old Republican issue
yet again, merely alienated Catholic votes.

The two principal trade unions CGT and CFDT were drawn into
the conflict between the parties of the left. The CGT, whose
leadership has been Communist since 1945, normally refrains from
the direct advice to its members to vote Communist. This time
its leader Georges Séguy (a member of the PCF *bureau politique*)
came out strongly for the PCF, took its side in the dispute over
the *Programme Commun*, attacked the Socialists, and campaigned
hard for a Communist vote - to the indignation of its executive
members who were not Communists. The CFDT, for its part, though
inclined to the Socialists, tried to bring the warring parties
together and to persuade them to desist from electoral suicide.

d. The Speeches of President Giscard d'Estaing

In the Fifth Republic the most prestigious political leader
is always the Head of State. Presidents of the Republic ostensibly cut themselves off from party politics, and certainly they
take pains not to descend into the vulgar arena of partisan cut-
and-thrust. Nonetheless successive Presidents, successive
majorités, and successive electorates have regarded Presidential
elections as the moment when the Head of the Executive and chief
initiator of public policy was to be chosen. In consequence it
would be absurd for a President to pretend he was an a-political
constitutional monarch. Presidential supremacy, furthermore,
depends to a large extent on the existence of a parliamentary
majority prepared to countenance presidential supremacy. So a
President of the Republic cannot be benignly indifferent to the
outcome of a Parliamentary election. On the other hand both the
dignity of his office and the fact that he might have to work
with a new majority dictate some care over the manner of any
presidential intervention. De Gaulle and Pompidou both declared
in various ways their unwillingness to work with a majority composed of Socialists and Communists, both used their 'non-political'
presidential prerogative to address the nation after the close of
the campaign on the eve of poll. Giscard d'Estaing followed the
second but not the first tradition. He played an extremely important part in the campaign.

In the first place it was he who, asthe constitution lays
down, determined the date of the election. If he had done what
his Prime Minister of the day, Jacques Chirac, had wanted and
opted for an earlier dissolution the left might very well have
won. Secondly he ruled out, repeatedly and also to the annoy-
ance of Chirac, the option of his own resignation if the left
won. This meant that the *majorité* could not, if it was concerned
with honesty, claim with great conviction that constitutional
chaos would follow a victory by the left. However it did mean
that the President, had he been faced with a victorious left,
to whose policies he would to some extent have had to adapt himself, would have remained *maître du jeu*. In particular he would
retain the vital presidential prerogative of choosing the date of

the next election - when his new left-wing government was at its most unpopular no doubt! In the third place he made two extremely adroit speeches during the election campaign which may well have had a decisive impact on the result.

The first speech was made at Verdun-sur-le-Doubs on January 27 - six weeks before the election. Addressing himself warmly to *'mes chères françaises et mes chers français'*, he asked the country to make the 'right choice' (*le bon choix*). It was not as party leader, naturally, that the President was suggesting that the *'bon choix'* was for the country to renew its confidence in the present government. In addition

> 'it is my duty to tell you again what I think of the *Programme Commun* - because it is a question not of electoral argument but of the fate of the French economy. The application in France of a programme of collectivist inspiration would plunge France into economic disorder . . . You may of course choose the *Programme Commun*. That is your right. But if you choose it, it will be applied. Don't think that the President of the Republic has, under the constitution, the means to stop it. And I would have failed in my duty if I had not warned you'.

That gave the country something to think about.

As the election came closer the question was whether or not the President would speak again to the nation and whether he would choose the eve of the first ballot or the second. His predecessor Georges Pompidou had chosen the eve of the second ballot in 1973 to make a very direct appeal:

> 'The choice is simple . . . on one side Marxist communism and the allies it has secured for itself, on the other everyone else. On one side a society which is ignorant of or which suppresses the liberty of the individual, political freedom, and the right to own one's own property, and which submits the life of each person to the authority of a totalitarian administration. On the other a free society . . .,'

Giscard d'Estaing, choosing the eve of the first ballot, abstained completely from caricatures of this kind. In one of the most skilful pronouncements of his Presidency he appealed to

reason. The three issues were the government of France (with
what partners and on what programme did the aspirant parties
propose to govern), the economy, which would be thrown back into
crisis by the 'massive application of promises', and the inter-
national situation of France. 'An enfeebled France would be a
France that slipped backwards in the competition of nations . . .
back to the humiliating search for overseas credits . . . assur-
ing at a stroke the economic and monetary preponderance in Europe
of our powerful partner - Federal Germany'. 'Your choice, as I
have told you, will be respected with all the consequences it
entails. That is the democratic rule, but it is also the measure
of your immense responsibility'. It was not a partisan speech:
there was no crude anti-communism, there was no appeal to vote
for the *majorité* which would turn a defeat into a personal dis-
avowal; and it recognised the desire for change and renewal and
greater justice expressed by electors. Did the speech change
people's minds? The Sofres post-election opinion poll suggests
that about 2% of electors changed their vote to the *majorité* at
the last moment and about one-quarter of these specifically claim
to have made the decision after the President's broadcast. The
effect is difficult to quantify with certainty - but an effect it
undoubtedly had.

NOTES

(1) Le Monde Dossiers et Documents: Les élections législatives
     de mars 1978, pp. 73-4.

CHAPTER 5. THE FIRST BALLOT

a. Turnout

Participation by voters in French elections, both local and
national as Table 5.1 shows, has been on the increase in the
1970's. The second ballot of the 1974 Presidential elections established at 88% an all-time record turnout and voting at even
the local (cantonal) elections of 1976 was the most vigorous for
an election of this type since 1945. It was not surprising therefore that March 1978 set a new record for voting at a Parliamentary
election.

Table 5.1 Increasing electoral turnout in the 1970's
           (first ballot figures)

Presidential elections	1969	78.2%
	1974	84.9%
Cantonal elections	1970	61.8%
	1976	65.4%
Municipal elections	1971	75.2%
	1977	78.8%
Parliamentary elections	1973	81.3%
	1978	83.3%

Table 5.2 Turnout in national elections - 5th Republic

Parliamentary (1st ballot)		Presidential		
1958	77.1%	1965	1st ballot	85.0%
1962	68.7%		2nd ballot	84.5%
1967	81.1%	1969	1st ballot	78.2%
1968	80.0%		2nd ballot	69.1%
1973	81.3%	1974	1st ballot	84.9%
1978	83.3%		2nd ballot	89.9%

There were more registered voters than ever before - partly because the 18-21 year-olds had been enfranchised in 1974 in fulfilment of an election pledge made by President Giscard d'Estaing, partly through national population growth, and partly because, according to the calculations of Alain Lancelot[1], some 750,000 individuals previously non-registered, had gone to the trouble of completing registration. A record proportion of this record electorate voted at the first ballot and an even larger proportion - a new record - voted at the second. Corsica as usual had the worst record for abstentions with Paris City, and Marseille, and parts of the rural south-west, next but some way behind. Of the age-groups the newly-enfranchised young were, like their British counterparts, the greatest abstainers.

b.   Overall results   (Table 5.3)

The results of the first ballot show a 'swing' from the *majorité* (taken to include the 1973 Centrists who subsequently joined it) to the left of about 3.8%. With 49.6% in metropolitan France, the left reached its highest-ever share of the votes in the Fifth Republic, but it was well below what was needed for victory, and well below the 51-53% that had been predicted in the opinion polls. Various press commentaries reported that the left had a majority of votes at the first ballot. This was not so - the total score of the left remained obstinately stuck just below the magic figure of 50% - just as it had been in the 1974 Presidential election - just as it would a week later in the second ballot (see Table 6.4).

The Socialists gained the most votes - indeed 43% more people voted Socialist than in 1973 and the Socialist share of the vote was up by a fifth - and became the 'first party of France'. Nevertheless they had had greater expectations and the result was for them a disappointment. The Communist Party, as we reported in the last chapter, was the focal point of the election and there seems little doubt that its own style during the campaign, the emphasis given to it by the *majorité*, and the collapse of the credibility of the *Unicn de la Gauche* had the effect of

Table 5.3   Detailed Results - 1978

	FIRST BALLOT VOTE (metropolitan France only)				SEATS (metropolitan and overseas)	
	1973		1978		1973 (490 seats)	1978 (491 seats)
Electorate	29.9m		34.4m			
Abstentions	18.7%		16.6%			
Spoilt papers	1.8%		1.8%			
Valid votes	23.7m		28.1m			

	m. votes	%	m. votes	%		
Left						
PCF *	5.1	21.4	5.8	20.7	73	86
PS/MRG *	4.9	20.8	7.0	25.0	101	114
PS*	4.5	19.1	6.4	22.9	89	104
MRG	.4	1.8	.6	2.1	12	10
(programme commun)	(10.0)	(42.2)	(12.8)	(45.8)		
LO	.2	.8	.5	1.7	-	-
LCR	.1	.4	.1	.3	-	-
FA (PSU)*	.5	2.0	.3	1.0	1	-
Other ext. left			.04	.1	-	-
(Extreme left)	(.8)	(3.2)	(.8)	(3.1)		
Other left*	.1	.4	.1	.5	1	-
Total Left	10.9	45.8	13.9	49.3	176	200
Ecologists	-	-	.6	2.1	-	-
Choisir (Feminist)	-	-	.04	.1	-	-
Jobertistes	-	-	.1	.4	-	-
Dissident Gaullists	.02	-	.07	.2	-	-
Réformateurs**	3.1**	13.1**	-	-	34**	-
Majorité						
UDF	-	-	6.0	21.4	-	138
PR	1.6	6.8	3.0	10.7	55	69
CDS	-	-	1.5	5.3	-	36
Radicals	-	-	.6	2.1	-	8
Other	-	-	.9	3.3	-	25.
RPR	6.1	25.7	6.3	22.5	183	150
Other *Majorité*	1.1	4.2	.6	2.0	35	2
Total *Majorité*	8.8	36.7	12.9	45.9	273	290
Extreme Right	.1	.5	.1	.5	-	-
Others	.9	3.9	.4	1.5	7	1

* PCF and PS figures include non-party candidates endorsed by them: PCF endorsed
  2 dissident Gaullists and 2 FA (PSU); PS endorsed 2 'other left'.
** *Réformateurs* (Centre Democrats and Radicals, 1973) joined the *majorité* after
  the 1974 Presidential election.

alienating from the left some moderate voters who had expressed
to opinion polls the intention of voting Socialist. The PCF
itself had a mixed election: it won its highest-ever number of
seats in the Fifth Republic[2] but it lost ground in terms of its
share of the votes, especially in its heartland the Paris region.
Table 5.4 incidentally shows that it still takes far more votes
on average to elect a Communist *député* than a *député* of any other
party. However its main campaign aim was fully achieved: to
check the loss of its own voters to the Socialist Party and to
prevent the elimination of its own strong candidates (including
députés seeking re-election) by Socialist candidates. Table 6.2
in the next chapter amplifies this point.

The *majorité* as a whole had considerable cause for satisfaction. Very limited damage was sustained. The nightmare of a
victory by the left was banished by the results of the first
ballot. Nearly all ministers and *députés* seeking re-election
were strongly placed. The UDF, rapidly formed a few weeks before
the election by the 'non-RPR' parties of the *majorité*, had become
one of the 'big four' with over 20% of the votes cast and had
proved once again the force of the Fifth Republic's basic electoral law that there is considerable advantage to any party or
candidate who is identified with the President of the Republic.
The leader of the RPR, finally, had the satisfaction of seeing
that his promise of returning to the Palais Bourbon at the head
of an army of 150 *députés* would be fulfilled. The Gaullists who,
at the beginning of the Giscard d'Estaing presidency, were being
written off by the opinion polls, were still the largest party of
the *majorité*. Table 5.4 throws some light on the strength of RPR
candidates.

The table also shows that it was not a good election for the
minor parties. The Ecologists came nowhere near the 5 or 7% that
was at one time predicted for them. Neither a doubling of the
number of candidates, nor the reduction of the voting age, helped
the extreme left to better its 1973 score. Within the two major
alliances the two fragments of the old Radical Party - MRG on the
left, the official Radical Party in the *majorité* - revealed themselves to be extremely feeble. Their performance is really worse

Table 5.4   Political parties: Average votes per candidate and
votes per seat (metropolitan)

	Votes per Candidate	Votes per seat
RPR	15800	44800
UDF*	15500	45500
PR	15300	45700
CDS	13800	46900
Radicals	8500	74200
PS	14500	57400
PCF	12300	79800
MRG	5000	60300

Minor parties:

Ecologists	2600
PSD (ex-Socialists)	2500
FA (PSU)	1400
Breton autonomists	1200
Jobertistes	1100
LO (Extreme left)	1000
Dissident Gaullists	900
Choisir (Feminist)	700
Extreme right	600
LCR (Extreme left)	500
Other Extreme left	300

* includes endorsed MDSF, CNIP, DC etc., and endorsed candidates with unspecified party affiliation.

than Table 5.4 suggests. Two-thirds of all the 600,000 MRG votes went to those 30 MRG candidates who had the support of the PS and no Socialist rival. The other 92 candidates, who were competing with Socialists, could only manage an average of just over 2000 votes each or 2% - well below the Ecologists. It was the same for the *majorité* Radicals. Nearly a half of their 600,000 votes came from the 16 Radicals, officially endorsed by the UDF, who either won their seats or at least contested the second ballot. The remainder, who were also endorsed for the UDF for the most part, only averaged about 6000 votes each.

The number of *députés* elected or re-elected at the first ballot was about average at 68. Table 5.5 shows that only the landslide of 1968 differed markedly from the normal and also that most of those elected at the first ballot are from the *majorité*. This is mainly because the strongly entrenched local notable is more frequently a member of the *majorité*, especially in areas like the Maine-et-Loire or Alsace or overseas France where first ballot elections are especially common. Another factor is that the left vote is invariably split at the first ballot between Socialists and Communists. Thus, apart from a handful of impregnable Communist strongholds, it is very rare for a candidate of the left to get over 50% in the first round. The table also shows that members of the *majorité*, despite the increased number of 'primaries' had an easier time in terms of first ballot elections than in 1973 and the Communists a more difficult time. Thirteen members of the government, including the Prime Minister, were elected at the first ballot.

Table 5.5   Members elected at first ballot

	1967	1968	1973	1978
Majorité	68	154	48	63*
Communists	8	6	8	4
Socialists	2	1	2	1
Total	78	161	58	68

* 31 RPR, 32 UDF and others

Some members were not elected at the first ballot but they might just as well have been for the new '12½% rule' eliminated all their opponents. No candidate who received the support of less than 12½% of the constituency's registered electorate is allowed to contest the second ballot. The only exception to that is when the strict application of the rule would leave only one candidate. Thus in Paris 2 the Socialist candidate was entitled to contest the second ballot though he had fallen below 12½% at the first. There were a number of cases however when the only candidates eligible for the second ballot were both from the *majorité* or both from the left. However both alliances follow the principle that there shall be a single candidate at the second ballot. Thus the *majorité* was completely eliminated from 5 constituencies but Socialists and Communists declined to fight it out at the second ballot and only the candidate who had done best at the first ballot went into the second. Thus Georges Marchais, the PCF leader, for instance, was the sole candidate at the second ballot in his constituency - where he scored 100% of the votes cast (though abstentions increased by 7000 and a further 20,000 voters took the trouble to cast a blank or spoiled ballot!). The left was completely eliminated from 8 constituencies. In 3 of them a sole candidate representing the *majorité* was permitted to gather 100% of the second ballot votes, but in the other 5 rival candidates of the *majorité* continued to fight it out.[3]

c. The Parties

Within the general trends - Socialist gains, Communist losses, *majorité* down but well-placed for victory - outlined at the beginning of this chapter, certain details are worth noting.

(i) PCF

The Communist share of the vote declined but it declined unevenly. Overall, at 20.7%, the PCF had one of its three worst elections since the war: 1958, 1968, 1978 - a crisis every ten years. The decline was uneven, however, amongst different age groups in the population, in different regions, and in particular constituencies.

As far as age-groups are concerned, the PCF benefitted from the extension of the franchise to the under-21's, 29% of whom voted Communist, and this masked the greater decline among the over-21's. Regionally the decline of the PCF was most marked in the Paris conurbation, from 27.1% in 1973 to 24.2% in 1978 - the continuation of a trend which had already began in the late 1960's. However the PCF actually increased its share of the vote, as Table 5.10 shows, in 9 of the 22 regions notably in traditional Socialist and radical bastions such as the North, the Midi-Pyrenees, the Limousin, or Corsica. In particular constituencies the PCF suffered, like other parties, from new candidates replacing familiar *députés*. A good example was the loss of the constituency in Nice held for many years by the *doyen* of the Assemblée, the 88 year-old Virgile Barel. The average effect of candidate replacement is shown in Table 5.6.

Table 5.6   Effect of change of candidates in Communist seats

Out of 73 Communist seats won in 1973

1978:	58 same candidate	15 new candidate
Communist vote declines in	62% of seats	93% of seats
Average Communist decline	-0.7%	-4.5%

Also worth noting is the particularly disastrous decision of the PCF not to present candidates in certain constituencies. In Val d'Oise I and Alpes-Maritimes 2 the Party supported dissident Gaullists. In Yvelines 4 and Rhône 6 it supported PSU candidates. The effect of liberating its supporters from the simple recommendation to vote Communist cost on average a decline of 8% compared to the Communist vote in 1973.

(ii)   The Socialists and MRG

The PS became in 1978 the leading party of the left for the first time since 1936. Presaged by local elections in 1976 and

1977, by by-elections and by opinion polls since 1974, this is an
important new phenomenon. Most of the gains achieved by the left
as a whole in the 1970's were Socialist gains. However, like
Communist losses, Socialist gains were uneven.

This unevenness is particularly noticeable in regional com-
parisons. The 'nationalisation' of political life has meant that
Socialist gains have been particularly marked in areas where traditionally it has been weak. In strongly Catholic regions like
Alsace and Brittany, as Table 5.10 shows, the Socialist vote increased considerably - over 7 percentage points - and continues a
trend which was revealed in 1973 and in the Presidential elections
of 1974. In Brittany the PS/MRG share of the vote is now the
same as its national average: 25%. As we note later in this chapter, this is not because church-going Catholics have started to
vote Socialist (see Table 5.11) but because France is becoming
more secular. In addition the PS has become a serious rival to
the PCF in the Paris region where Communist losses have been more
than compensated by a 6% Socialist gain. In three Southern regions, however, where Socialists have been traditionally strong,
the Party has declined slightly: Languedoc, Limousin and Provence-
Côte d'Azur. In some Socialist strongholds, the decline, like
that of the PCF in its own territory, is explained by a change of
candidate. In 12 of 17 constituencies where a Socialist *député*
sortant was not seeking re-election, the Socialist vote fell, and
the average drop was 1.5%. In some strongholds the phenomenon of
Socialist decline is explicable by the crumbling of the anti-
Communist element of the Socialist vote: voting Socialist had
ceased to be the best way to keep the Communists out. The case
of the northern industrial town of Cambrai is illuminating. From
1968 to 1978 the PCF gained 3.5% becoming the principal party of
the left in 1973. The Socialist vote has collapsed over the same
period by 11%.

One further point remains to be examined - why Socialist
gains (+ 4% from 1973) were so much lower than the gains predicted
in opinion polls. The comparison of immediate pre-electoral and
post-electoral polls gives an insight into a potential Socialist
electorate that abandoned the left on election day (Table 5.7).

We have already suggested a number of explanatory factors - the
fact that some potential Socialist supporters did not 'in their
heart of hearts' really want the left to win (Table 2.3),
the eve-of-poll speech by President Giscard d'Estaing, the effect
of the anti-Socialist campaign by the Communist Party.

Table 5.7   Lost votes of the PS

	Pre-electoral opinion polls (end Feb.)	Post-electoral opinion polls	
	PS%	PS%	
Total electorate	28	25	-3
Sex - men	30	25	-5
women	26	25	-1
Age - 18-24	26	25	-1
- 25-34	30	24	-6
- 35-49	31	25	-6
- 51-64	28	24	-4
Occupation -			
farmers	24	17	-7
self-employed	22	23	+1
professional, senior management	20	15	-5
clerical workers	35	29	-6
manual workers	32	27	-5
retired, etc.	25	26	+1

(Source: J. Jaffré - 'L'opinion publique et les élections
législatives', *Projet*, juin 1978)

As Jérome Jaffré notes, this ebb-tide flows in favour both
of the PCF and the *majorité*: for the Communists amongst manual
workers and the 25-34 age group, for the *majorité* amongst the
34-49 age group, clerical workers, management and farmers.

(iii) The *Majorité*

The RPR stood up well to competition from its newly-unified
rivals and its leader seems to have been both a help and a

hindrance: his dynamic and pugnacious style certainly raised the morale of *majorité* voters, but his attacks on the President, the Prime Minister and the other *majorité* parties seem to have displeased public opinion. All in all, however, the RPR candidates, *députés* seeking re-election and well-established local notables, generally identified with the *majorité*, were worth more in terms of votes than the RPR party itself or Jacques Chirac. The RPR's 22.5% of votes cannot be compared with any previous result because there exists no precedent for this bipolar restructuring of the *majorité* between RPR and the rest. However one can note that in Paris, the RPR improved very slightly on its lead in the municipal elections but, conversely, declined in the 34 constituencies where, in 1973, it had already faced 'primaries' against other parties in the *majorité*.

In seeking to explain why some candidates of the *majorité* score better than others at the first ballot, the principal variable is not the party they belong to but 'notability'. A well-entrenched *député*, who is also mayor of a town in the constituency and possibly a *conseiller général* as well, is very hard to beat. Table 5.8 demonstrates clearly how the better-known candidates of either RPR or UDF have an immense advantage over their rivals. There were however some exceptions to this rule as *majorité députés* and other notables were occasionally eliminated not by the left but by their partners (see Table 6.2 in the next chapter). On balance UDF candidates showed the greater capacity to eliminate RPR partners better-known than they. Table 5.9 shows the route to the second ballot for *majorité* candidates.

Table 5.8 'Notability' and *majorité* 'primaries'

	Average lead of UDF
UDF candidate much better known than RPR	+24%
UDF candidate slightly better known than RPR	+10.5%
UDF and RPR candidates equally well-known	-0.8%
RPR candidate slightly better known than UDF	-10.3%
RPR candidate much better known than UDF	-21.5%

(Source: J. Jaffrè in H. Penniman, ed.: France at the Polls - II, Washington DC, 1978).

Table 5.9   Notability and *majorité* second ballot candidatures

	RPR	UDF
More 'notable' than ally	91	86
'Open' primaries	61	45
Less 'notable' than ally	16	27
No primary	53	33

The principal point about the UDF - the immense electoral advantage in the Fifth Republic to any party identified with the Head of State - has already been made. The part of the UDF most closely identified as *Giscardien* - the Republican Party (PR - formerly RI) - emerged as its strongest element. Half of all UDF candidates were PR (see Table 3.4, page 41) and they received 3 million of the UDF's 6 million votes. The capacity of the UDF, as a 'moderate' political force, to attract extra second ballot votes, will be examined in the next chapter.

The *majorité* declined in all regions of France except those old fortresses of the left, Provence and the Limousin. The UDF is now the leading party of the *majorité* in 10 regions (see Table 5.10) - its importance being particularly marked in Lower Normandy, Lorraine, Rhône-Alps, and the Auvergne. Over the decade that has elapsed since 1967 the most significant regional change is the loss by the *majorité* of its totally dominant position in the traditionally strong catholic regions of the West and Alsace-Lorraine.

(iv) Marginal groups

Squeezed between the two blocs of the *majorité* and left, the marginal groups gathered a very thin harvest, as Table 5.3 shows. The Ecologists, who attracted a lot of interest before the election, finished with 2-2½%, (depending upon whether or not one counts the votes cast for Ecologist candidates under the banner of *Front Autogestionnaire*). This in some ways was not the derisory total it appears at first sight. With candidates in less than half of all constituencies, they were generally leaders of the little band of minor candidates. If one examines the 19 constituencies where Ecologists had more than 7% of the vote, whether in

Table 5.10

Election Results - Regional Summary - Main Political Groups - 1973 and 1978 (% of 1st ballot vote and seats won)

	PCF 1973 %	PCF 1973 S	PCF 1978 %	PCF 1978 S	PS/MRG 1973 %	PS/MRG 1973 S	PS/MRG 1978 %	PS/MRG 1978 S	Maj. + Centre 1973 %	Maj. + Centre 1973 S	Total maj.* 1978 %	Total maj.* 1978 S	Majorités 1978 UDF 1978 %	UDF 1978 S	RPR 1978 %	RPR 1978 S
Champagne (12)	22.4	-	22.8	2	20.7	2	23.0	-	50.0	10	48.0	10	21.1	5	26.4	5
Picardy (15)	28.0	3	27.7	6	18.6	2	21.7	3	44.9	10	42.3	6	20.1	2	23.0	4
North (37)	26.9	12	27.7	14	26.6	15	28.2	17	40.5	10	38.1	10	16.5	2	20.1	4
Upper Normandy (14)	25.7	-	26.0	4	16.8	2	22.7	2	50.8	10	43.9	8	20.1	4	22.7	4
Lower Normandy (13)	11.7	-	10.7	-	17.7	2	22.7	2	64.6	10	57.9	11	38.0	7	19.0	4
Brittany (25)	16.0	-	14.8	1	17.1	3	24.8	4	58.2	21	54.4	20	24.6	9	22.6	11
Loire Country (26)	11.7	-	12.2	1	19.0	2	24.6	3	61.8	23	55.2	22	24.5	10	30.5	12
Paris Region (83)	27.1	31	24.2	27	14.9	3	21.0	5	46.5	49	44.0	51	18.1	18	24.0	33
Alsace (13)	7.9	-	6.6	-	12.4	-	19.8	-	73.3	13	63.5	13	25.4	6	33.6	7
Lorraine (21)	16.9	2	16.9	3	18.5	1	26.1	2	57.4	18	50.7	16	27.2	10	19.7	6
Franche-Comté (9)	14.0	-	14.9	-	27.4	3	30.7	3	51.4	6	47.6	6	24.5	4	16.5	1
Burgundy (15)	19.3	-	18.2	-	26.0	5	29.6	6	51.4	10	45.6	6	16.3	4	24.5	4
Centre (20)	21.3	1	20.7	-	18.7	2	23.9	1	53.2	17	47.7	19	23.5	8	22.8	11
France - North (303)	21.3	51	20.4	58	18.8	42	23.9	48	51.3	207	47.2	197	21.6	89	23.0	106
Poitou Charentes (14)	18.0	-	17.1	1	21.1	2	27.9	6	51.3	12	48.5	7	24.1	3	22.6	3
Limousin (8)	29.9	3	30.4	4	25.3	2	24.4	1	42.2	2	38.6	3	4.5	-	30.8	3
Aquitaine (24)	17.5	2	18.0	2	27.1	9	30.7	14	47.6	13	44.1	8	13.6	1	28.7	8
Midi-Pyrenees (22)	16.3	1	18.0	-	31.3	15	34.2	18	46.1	7	40.8	4	15.6	1	21.5	3
Auvergne (13)	20.2	2	19.2	3	24.4	4	26.9	3	52.8	7	46.1	8	28.1	5	17.5	3
Rhône-Alps (42)	19.6	6	18.9	3	20.8	7	25.2	12	51.9	31	45.7	27	27.0	19	16.7	8
Languedoc (16)	28.2	8	27.7	7	27.0	8	25.8	5	44.3	3	37.1	4	23.5	4	15.7	1
Provence-Côte d'Azur (28)	28.2	8	26.9	9	22.3	9	22.0	5	47.7	10	42.6	14	21.9	11	19.4	3
Corsica (4)	14.5	-	16.0	-	27.5	2	29.0	-	53.6	1	52.7	1	18.1	-	33.3	4
France - South (171)	21.6	22	21.4	28	24.6	59	27.0	64	46.6	85	43.0	79	20.8	43	21.6	35
Metropolitan France (474)	21.4	73	20.7	86	20.8	101	25.0	112	49.8	292	45.9	276	21.4	132	22.5	141
Overseas France (17)	-	-	-	-	-	2	-	2	-	15	-	15	-	6	-	9
Total (491)	-	73	-	86	-	103	-	114	-	307	-	291	-	138	-	150

Paris or the Provinces (where Alsace and Lower Normandy were their
best regions), 'the Ecologist vote seems to reflect the preoccupations of the middle-income and affluent sections of the population worried about urbanisation, development, or, of course,
nuclear power stations'.[4] Young and generally coming from relatively favoured social backgrounds - in Paris the distribution of the
Ecologist vote corresponds perfectly with the proportion of tea-
chers in the population - the ecological electorate seems to be
composed of two distinct groups. The first is a highly politicised
element originating from the extreme left but, by contrast, the
second has the neo-Poujadist outlook of the politically indifferent.

The failure of the extreme left to improve its 1973 score,
despite the support of 12% of the age group 18-20 and despite
having twice as many candidates this time, is directly related
to the presence of the Ecologists. To analyse these two marginal
electorates separately is to conceal both their complementary
character and their new importance - 5 or 6% - on the left of the
French political spectrum. Within the extreme left, the *Front
Autogestionnaire* based on the PSU reached 3% in 40 constituencies,
Lutte Ouvrière in 32, the *Ligue Communiste* in none. On the
extreme left, *Lutte Ouvrière* had the most clearly working-class
electorate.

The meagre results obtained by the remnants of opposition
centrism - Michel Jobert's *Mouvement Démocrate*, Eric Hintermann's
group of dissident ex-Socialists the PSD, or Gisèle Halimi's fem-
inist movement *Choisir* - require no special commentary.

d. Sociology of voting behaviour

The sociological characteristics of the four principal electorates, PC, PS, UDF, RPR (see Table 5.11), show a similar pattern
to previous elections. The left is supported by a majority of
men, of the under-35's, of clerical and manual workers. The
majorité leads among women, the over-50's, farmers, employers and
the professions. However some special characteristics and interesting new developments are worth noting.

TABLE 5.11   The 1978 electorate - vote by social categories
(% of first ballot votes - major parties only)

	% of each category that voted:-			
	PCF	PS/MRG	UDF	RPR
Total electorate	21	25	21	22
Sex -				
Men (48% of population)	24	25	19	20
Women (52%)	19	25	22	24
Occupation (head of family) -				
Farmers (9%)	9	17	33	31
Self-employed (7%)	14	23	25	26
Professional, management (9%)	9	15	27	30
Clerical workers (19%)	18	29	14	20
Manual workers (28%)	36	27	16	14
Retired, etc. (27%)	17	26	25	26
Age -				
18-24* (15%)	28	25	17	15
25-34 (20%)	26	24	18	17
35-49 (25%)	19	25	20	24
50-64 (20%)	20	24	22	23
65+ (20%)	15	25	27	28
Religion -				
Regular church-going RC (17%)	2	13	39	31
Occasional church-going RC (15%)	11	20	28	33
Non-church-going RC (49%)	24	30	17	20
No religion (14%)	49	29	4	6
Voted in 1974 -				
Giscard d'Estaing (51%)	2	8	37	39
Mitterrand (49%)	42	44	5	2

* 9% of age group 18-24 voted extreme-left (3% of electorate as a whole)

(Source: SOFRES sondage post-électoral, Nouvel Observateur)

(i) <u>Age</u>

The link between age and voting is perfect: the *majorité* was supported by 32% in the 18-24 age group, 35% in the 25-34, 44% in the 35-49, 45% in the 50-64, and 55% of those over 65. The reduction of the voting age from 21 to 18 calls for a special look at the votes of the new 18-20 year-old electorate (Table 5.12). Here the 4 main parties were by no means equally successful, and furthermore, alongside the support for the main parties (29% - PCF, 22% - PS, 28% - *majorité* and right) one finds the existence of what has been called an *'électorat critique'* an electorate, left-wing in orientation, which is critical of all the big parties and is attracted to the groups of the extreme-left and the new forms of *contestation* - especially Ecologist. This *électorat critique* amounts to no less than 21% of this age-group.

Table 5.12   The vote of the 18-20 age group in 1978 (1st ballot)

PCF	29%
Extreme left	12%
PS/MRG	22%
Ecologists and other opposition	9%
UDF	11%
RPR	14%
Other *majorité* and right	3%

It is naturally very difficult to say what will become in a few years' time of these young electors who in such large numbers today reject both the *programme commun* and the *majorité*. As age begets moderation perhaps they will find in the PS the more moderate representative of their *contestation*, especially as this *contestation* has, both in the language of the extreme-left and the Ecologists, strong overtones of anti-communism. The PCF can be reasonably encouraged by its support in this age-group, which matches the Party's rapid membership growth in the period up to 1977, though it may not be sufficient to offset the traditional tendency for the Communist vote to decline as age increases.

The *majorité* will find plenty to worry it in these figures.
Even if it gained the support of the young who abstained in 1978
(at one in four, the highest proportion of any age-group) and of
some of the Ecologists and supporters of the left, growing wise
with advancing years, it nonetheless faces the future with a serious handicap.

France is probably the only country in Europe today where
age and electoral behaviour are so closely linked, and where the
balance in favour of the left is so marked among young electors.
It is difficult to explain this phenomenon. Does it signify a
desire for change in a country which has not known the alternation of power? Does it result from the apolitical character of
many French households where the absence of political conversations within the family and the widespread ignorance about paren-
tal voting behaviour make the transmission of the family's political values very difficult? The figures for age and electoral
behaviour give no indication that the rise of the left is at an
end.

(ii) <u>Sex</u>

The important fact to underline is not that a majority of
men vote for the left and of women for the *majorité*, but the pro-
gressive reduction of this difference between the sexes. In 1967
65% of women voted for the *majorité* and the centre, and only 48%
of men. This gap was down to 9 points in 1973, to 7 in 1974, and
to 6 points in 1978. It is in the Communist electorate that the
gap remains strongest: 25% of men voted Communist but only 19% of
women. This is explained by the fact that there are fewer women
manual workers, and more women are responsive to the Catholic
religion.

(iii) <u>Occupation</u>

More than two-thirds of manual workers voted for the opposition. This is in sharp contrast to the period of General de
Gaulle's presidency when the left was supported by only about half
of the working-class (54% in 1968 for example). In 1973-74 the

left recovered its dominant position in the working-class and this was confirmed in 1978. THe PCF is the largest party in this social category (36%) and half of all Communist voters are working-class. It is also worth recalling that among voters deciding at the last moment not to vote Socialist (see Table 5.6) there were quite a number of workers returning to the Communist fold.

The left also predominates among clerical workers - especially the Socialist Party. It was in this category and among senior management and the professions that the PS made the most progress in 1978 and inflicted the greatest losses on the right (see Table 5.13):

Table 5.13   Occupational category and the decline of the *majorité* 1973-78

	Maj. (% points)
Clerical workers, junior management	-14
Senior management, professions	-13
Self-employed	- 6
Retired, etc.	- 3
Farmers	- 2
Manual workers	- 1
(Electorate as a whole)	(- 4)

Among wage and salary-earners the left is particularly strongly supported by union members. However the difference between the voting behaviour of CGT and CFDT members is remarkable. Table 5.14 shows the preponderance of the PCF and the non-existence of support for the *majorité* among CGT members. The CGT Communist vote is in fact 5 points up compared to 1973 - indicating perhaps the success of the strong and unprecedented CGT campaign in favour of the Communist Party. With the CFDT membership, the right, the extreme-left, and, above all, the Socialists (+6 points from 1973) perform somewhat better.

TABLE 5.14   Union membership and voting behaviour, 1978

	CGT	CFDT
PCF	63%	23%
Extreme-left	2%	11%
PS/MRG	28%	36%
UDF	1%	15%
RPR	4%	10%
Other	2%	5%
	100%	100%

(Source: SOFRES)

The *majorité* revealed its traditional strength among farmers, traders, and the more affluent sectors of society. An interesting fact is the extraordinary similarity between the electoral composition of its two principal parties: same occupational structure, same age pyramid. The days of Gaullism's appeal to the working-class, despite the protestations to the contrary by RPR activists, are well and truly over. More workers and their families voted UDF than RPR. The similarity of the RPR and UDF electorates should not surprise us too much because, as we have already noted, the main explanation of the relative success of a UDF or RPR candidate is local 'notability'. There were four main political forces in the first ballot but there are only three identifiable electorates[5].

(iv) Religion

It is well-known that in France Catholic religion and the regularity of church-going constitute the best predictive variable in electoral behaviour[6]. Thus a greater proportion of senior management and professional people who have no religious faith vote Communist than of working-class Catholics who are regular church-goers.

The growth of the Socialist Party, its attraction for various left-wing Christian groups, its close identification with the CFDT which, up to 1964, had been specifically the union for

Christian workers, the success of the Socialists in local elections in 1976 and 1977 in regions with a strong Catholic tradition, led many observers to cast doubts on the persistence of
the old relationship between churchgoing and voting for the right
or centre. Table 5.11 demonstrates clearly that the relationship
is as strong as ever. 80% of regular church attenders (mass at
least once a month) vote for the *majorité* or the right. By the
same token 88% of those claiming no religious affiliation vote
for the left, with 49% voting Communist.

In fact it is not a change in the relationship between
religion and voting that explains the Socialist gains in Catholic
regions but the slow but regular decline of religious practice
in a changing and increasingly urban society. Almost three-
quarters of all Frenchmen now live in towns with over 2000 population (59% in 1954) and regular churchgoing has declined during
the Fifth Republic from around 25% to 16% today.

Nearly all Frenchmen who claim any religious attachment are
Catholics - but not all. There are a few hundred thousand Protestants and about 100,000 Jews who practise their religions. A
majority of both groups voted for the non-Communist left[7]: Jews
(55% plus 1% for the PCF and 33% for the *majorité*), Protestants
(40%, 4% PCF, 40% *majorité*).

The first ballot of a French parliamentary election is an
opportunity to measure the strength of the different political
parties and, thanks largely to the very detailed post-electoral
opinion polls carried out by SOFRES, to analyse the sociological
characteristics of voting behaviour. However the political importance of the first ballot lies in the way it prepares the ground
for the second ballot which will decide the election. When we
say that the left lost the election at the first ballot, we mean
that its performance at the first was not a sufficient spring-
board for victory at the second. One of the features of the 1978
election which has been one of the principal themes of this book
was the ferocious rivalry between the partners in the two big
alliances. The rivalry was for access to the second ballot. The
particularly aggressive style of both PCF and RPR in their

dealings with their partners is explained in large part by the fear each had of seeing its strong candidates and even *députés* eliminated not by its adversaries but by its allies. The outcome of this rivalry in terms of second ballot candidatures and final results will be examined in the next chapter.

NOTES

(1) *Projet*, juin 1978.

(2) The PC won 6 seats from the PS and in these constituencies its candidates made genuine gains (PC +2%, PS -4%). In 16 seats it won from the *majorité*, however, the left's gains in first ballot votes compared with 1973 (+3.5% on average) were all made by Socialists!

(3) *Majorité* eliminated by the 12½% rule in the following constituencies:-

> Seine St. Denis 2 (PCF)
> Val de Marne 1 (PCF)
> Pas de Calais 10 (PCF)
> Pas de Calais 12 (PS)
> Aude 2 (PS)

Left eliminated by 12½% rule:-

No second ballot contest within *majorité* - Paris 20 (UDF)
Paris 21 (UDF)
Hauts-de-Seine 6 (Ind-Maj)

Second ballot contest within *majorité* - Paris 4
Paris 6
Paris 22
Paris 23
Manche 2

(In all these five cases the RPR led at the first ballot and won at the second).

(4) Roland Cayrol 'naissance d'un électorat critique', le dossier des législatives 1978, le Matin de Paris.

(5) Formula borrowed from J. Jaffré in *Projet*, juin 1978.

(6) See G. Michelat and M. Simon Classe, religion, et politique, Paris: Presses de la Fondation Nationale des Sciences Politique, and Editions Sociales, 1977.

(7) Le Point, 30 janvier 1978.

CHAPTER 6. THE SECOND BALLOT

        The second ballot in a French election is, theoretically
speaking, a bright new morning.   There is no compulsion on the
elector to vote the way he did a week before, to follow the sug-
gestions of the party he normally supports, or even to vote at
all. Alain Lancelot[1] has shown that it is not entirely the same
individuals who vote in the two ballots: some abstainers at one
ballot are voters at the other. In addition the French voter
can do what his British counterpart cannot do: cast a blank or
spoiled vote and, by having it recorded as such, register his
feelings about the candidates in general. However a bright new
morning has a way of turning into an ordinary sort of day and in
fact, in March 1978, the results of the second ballot pretty much
confirmed the trend indicated by the first. Participation in the
vote, in the constituencies involved in the second ballot, went
up from 83% to 84% - with differences, as we shall see, that depend on the type of constituency. The left held steady with
about 12½ million votes in each round while the *majorité* gained
over 1½ million votes from one ballot to the next. This is a familiar phenomenon in French elections (see Table 6.5) demonstra-
ting yet again that if the left wants to win a victory it must
have a substantial majority at the first ballot. The result was
an easy win for the outgoing government with a lead of 91 seats
over the opposition. The left won a few seats (24 net gains to
be precise) but there were none of the remarkable results we saw
in 1973 when the left and especially the Socialists were rolling
back the tide that had engulfed them in 1968. The cities in
Catholic France like Rennes or Angers which had fallen to the
left in the 1977 municipal elections remained firmly in pro-
government hands in 1978. In this chapter we shall concentrate
principally on three interesting facets of the second ballot and
on what they tell us of the strengths and weaknesses of the
country's main political forces: the candidates who got through
to the second ballot, the variations in abstentions in different
types of constituency, and the transfer of votes within alliances.

The rivalry between the two big alliances for places in the second ballot and hence for the chance to return to the Assembly with a large Parliamentary group has been one of the principal themes of this study. An analysis of the candidates who won through to the second ballot is therefore particularly interesting.

Table 6.1   SECOND BALLOT CANDIDATURES
             (Metropolitan France)

1978		1973	
RPR	221	UDR	309
UDF & other *Maj*	192*	RI/CDP/*Ref*+	110
PS/MRG	264**	PS/MRG	220
PCF	146	PCF	184

(* does not include 6 UDF who trailed behind RPR in first
     ballot but insisted nonetheless on challenging then
     unsuccessfully at the second)
(+ includes 18 *Réformateurs* - opposition centrists - who had
     second ballot support from the *majorité*)
(** includes a non-party candidate - Cornut-Gentille - with PS
     support)

Types of contest:

        Majorité - Opposition duels: 404

              RPR - PS/MRG   134
              UDF - PS/MRG   127
              RPR - PCF   81
              UDF - PCF   62

        Duels within *Majorité*:   5

        Triangular PS-RPR-UDF: 1

        No contest: 8

              PCF   3
              PS   2
              UDF   3

The practice of having *majorité* 'primaries' in most con-stituencies brought the *Giscardiens* almost equal to the RPR in the number of their second ballot candidatures whereas they had been widely separated in 1973. The PCF lost ground to the PS but

TABLE 6.2   SECOND BALLOT CANDIDATURES: RIVALRY WITHIN ALLIANCES
             (1978 candidatures compared to 1973 - metropolitan
             France)

        PCF eliminated by PS as second ballot candidate in

            1 seat held by PCF   (won by PS)[a]

            42 seats held by
                majorité   (12 won by PS)

        PS eliminated by PCF as second ballot candidate in

            7 seats held by PS   (6 won by PCF, 1 lost to
                                           majorité)[b]

            1 seat held by   (won by *majorité*)
                majorité

        RPR eliminated by UDF as second ballot candidate in

            17 seats held by RPR   (13 won by UDF, 4 lost to
                                           opposition)[c]

            33 seats held by   (9 won by UDF)
                opposition

        UDF eliminated by RPR as second ballot candidate in

            8 seats held by UDF   (6 won by RPR, 2 lost to
                                           opposition)[d]

            14 seats held by   (1 won by RPR)
                opposition

(a) Pas-de-Calais 9

(b) 2 *Députés sortants*: Alpes de Haute Provence 2, Nord 21.

     5 other PS seats: Ardennes 2, Bouches-du-Rhône 8, Gard 2,
     Vaucluse 2**, Haute-Vienne 3.

(c) 8 *Députés sortants*: Finistère 2, Haute-Marne 1, Oise 2*,
     Orme 3, Pas-de-Calais 4*, Haute-Savoie 3, Var 3,
     Val d'Oise 4.

     9 other RPR seats: Loiret 1, Mayenne 1, Marne 1, Hauts de
     Seine 12, Bas-Rhin 1, Bas-Rhin 4, Rhone 2, Vienne 1*, Vosges 2*

(d) 6 *Députés sortants*: Ain 1, Lot-et-Garonne 3*, Moselle 6,
     Paris 15, Rhône 2, Yvelines 5.

     2 other UDF seats: Gers 2*, Savoie 2.

     (** seat lost to *majorité*; * seats lost to opposition)

not nearly as much as they must have feared a year or two earlier
when PS candidates were regularly running ahead of quite well
entrenched Communists in the first ballot in local elections and
by-elections. In fact, as Table 6.2 shows, the PCF held on in
their own strongholds. They lost only one seat to the Socialists
but gained 7 at Socialist expense. One of the problems for a candidate in a French election is that he has to hold off a challenge
from or to eliminate his ally and then beat his adversary. As
Table 6.2 shows, sixteen *députés* seeking re-election were knocked
out by their allies (2 Socialists, 8 RPR, 6 UDF). Twelve newly-
elected Socialists had to beat a Communist and then the *majorité*,
9 UDF had to beat the Gaullists before beating the opposition,
and 1 RPR had to eliminate a *Giscardien* before defeating the
enemy.

We noted in chapter 5 the importance of 'notability' as a
variable in explaining which candidates of the *majorité*, RPR or
UDF won through to the second ballot. Table 3.3 also stressed
the importance of *implantation locale*: 83% of all *députés* seeking re-election, who also held local offices like Mayor or *Conseiller Général*, were re-elected.

Where 'notability' was roughly equal ('open' primaries)
the PS was conspicuously more attractive to the electorate than
the PCF and the RPR somewhat more successful than the UDF. This
slight advantage was redressed by the apparently greater capacity
of UDF candidates to eliminate RPR partners more 'notable' than
they (see Tables 5.7 and 5.8). There are other factors of course
which those tables do not show. For example most constituencies
with a strong tradition of voting Communist went on putting a
Communist top of the left whether he was well-known locally or
not. Equally, Socialists appear to predominate on the left in
the best constituencies of the *majorité* (see Table 6.8). On the
whole presence in the second ballot seems to be explained by a
combination of notability, local voting tradition, and the special appeal of parties on the way up - in 1978 the UDF and the PS.

The appeal of the UDF and the PS to voters in 1978 is
revealed further by an analysis of the way electoral participation
in the second ballot was different in different types of

constituency - a difference, as we shall see, that is mainly related to the candidates in the second ballot. Voting turnout, as we have reported, was up from 83% to 84% in constituencies where there was a second ballot, a phenomenon which in itself calls for some comment. Traditionally turnout declines between ballots as many voters find their favourite candidates eliminated and perhaps do not wish to make a choice between those that remain. However in the Parliamentary elections of 1973 and 1978 (and incidentally the Presidentials of 1974) - elections with a real possibility of a left-wing victory hence elections which were presented to the public as a 'choice of society', of fundamental importance to the economy, to the constitution, to freedom - turnout has actually increased at the second (see Table 6.3).

Table 6.3   Voting turnout: difference between ballots, 1967-78
            (constituencies where second ballot contests occurred)

	1st ballot %	2nd ballot %	Difference
1967	80.8	79.7	-1.1
1968	79.8	77.8	-2.0
1973	81.2	81.9	+0.6
1978	83.3	84.3	+1.0

(Source: J-L Parodi 'L'échec des gauches', Revue Politique et Parlementaire, mai 1978)

The predicted closeness of the result and the intensity of the campaign also clearly had their effect. The second ballot of 1974 was an all-time record at 88%, and the second ballot of 1978 an all-time record for Parliamentary elections. This increased turnout went to the aid principally of government supporters (Table 6.4) - as it usually does (Table 6.5).

This additional 'mobilisation' of voters occurred throughout the country - less so in the Paris region than anywhere else, less so in seats that were obviously safe for one side or the other than in seats that were not, more so in the most closely-contested marginals than in less marginal constituencies. In a

Table 6.4   RESULTS OF SECOND BALLOT
             (418 metropolitan constituencies with 2 ballots)

	1st ballot		2nd ballot	
Abstentions	16.1%		15.2%	
Spoilt papers	2.0%		2.4%	
Left	12.4m	50.1%	12.6m	49.5%
(PCF)		(21.3)		(18.7)
(PS/MRG)		(25.6)		(30.7)
(Ext. left)		(3.3)		(-)
Majorité	11.2m	45.0%	12.8m	50.5%
(RPR)		(22.1)		(26.0)
(UDF & other)		(22.9)		(24.5)
Others	1.2m	4.9%	-	-

Table 6.5   *Majorité* gains and left losses at second ballot
                                                    1967-78

             (constituencies with second ballot contests only)

	Majorité			Left		
	1st ballot %	2 nd ballot %	Difference	1st ballot %	2nd ballot %	Differen
1967	35.3	42.6	+7.3	45.5	46.4	+0.9
1968	41.0	48.8	+7.8	44.2	42.0	-2.2
1973	39.4	46.9	+7.5	47.5	47.0	-0.5
1978	45.0	50.5	+5.5	50.1	49.5	-0.6

(Source: J-L Parodi 'L'échec des gauches', op.cit.)

few constituencies turnout went down - especially of course those
where there was only one candidate at the second ballot or a duel
between two *majorité* candidates where the left had been completely eliminated at the first ballot. We have already noted that
where Georges Marchais stood as sole second ballot candidate turnout declined by 9 percentage points and a third of those who
went to vote cast spoiled ballots.[2] Equally in Paris 20 where a
sole candidate - *majorité* - was present turnout was down 13 points
and spoilt papers were a further 14%. The inter-*majorité* duel in
Paris 23 produced a turnout 10 points down and 16% spoilt papers.
In *majorité*-opposition duels, however, turnout normally increased
by an amount that varied according to the type of contest. The
number of spoilt ballot papers also frequently increased - especially where the candidate for the left was a Communist and even
more particularly where he was a well-known Communist and prominent member of the central committee. It did not seem to matter
whether such Communists were 'liberals' or hard-liners - they all
suffered equally. Spoilt papers increased by nearly 4000 in
Pierre Juquin's constituency (liberal) and by 2500 in Charles
Fiterman's (hard-line). Table 6.6 sheds some light on these aspects of differential participation. The UDF and the PS were the
greatest 'mobilisers' - turnout increased most where they were
presenting candidates and in UDF/PS contests the number of people
feeling impelled to spoil their votes dropped by comparison to
the first ballot. The more aggressive party of each camp - RPR
and PCF - was less able to galvanise electors into voting at the
second ballot, and their presence did more to make people cast
spoilt votes. For further evidence of the appeal of moderates,
see Table 6.7.

The final point to be analysed is the transfer of votes
within an alliance: the extent to which Socialist voters will vote
Communist at the second ballot when there is no Socialist candidate to which UDF voters will vote RPR and so on. Within the
majorité there seems to be no great problem: nearly all voters in
1978 seemed willing to rally behind the candidate still in the
lists against the left. As Table 6.7 shows, this is slightly
less true where the opposition candidate is a Socialist. On the

TABLE 6.6   DIFFERENTIAL VOTING TURNOUT - SECOND BALLOT
(Average votes per constituency - metropolitan France)

	Turnout (*votants*)	Valid votes (*suffrages exprimés*)	Spoilt papers (*blancs et nuls*)
A. Safe seats and marginal seats			
All seats*	+1400	+1100	+300
Safe seats (winner over 60%)	±0	- 300	+300
Marginals (winner under 51½%)	+2000	+1800	+200

(* all seats where second ballot was a duel *majorité-opposition*)

B. Type of second ballot contest (safe seats excluded)			
RPR/PS	+1600	+1600	±0
UDF/PS	+1850	+1950	-100
RPR/PCF	+1200	+ 350	+850
UDF/PCF	+1650	+ 850	+800

C. Presence in second ballot (safe seats excluded) of			
RPR	+1400	+1050	+350
UDF	+1800	+1550	+250
PS/MRG	+1700	+1750	- 50
PCF	+1400	+ 600	+800

left it has always been a handicap to present a Communist as
second ballot candidate because a lot of Socialist voters will
not vote Communist (44% in 1973 - a good year for unity - according to one estimate[3]).

Table 6.7   Transfer of votes between ballots

| | | \multicolumn{5}{c}{Second ballot vote for:-} | | | | |
First ballot vote for ↴		RPR	UDF	PS/MRG	PCF	Abstention etc
A. PCF/UDF duels	PS		23		65	12
	RPR		91		2	7
B. PCF/RPR duels	PS	10			73	17
	UDF	90			3	7
C. PS/UDF duels	PCF		3	98		2
	RPR		83	4		9
D. PS/RPR duels	PCF	3		94		3
	UDF	83		4		13

(Source: SOFRES - Sondage post-électoral, April 1978)

The same phenomenon clearly occurred in 1978. Practically all
Communist voters were willing to vote Socialist at the second
ballot if necessary. Table 6.7 reveals, however, that only 65%
of Socialist first ballot voters transferred to Communist at the
second if the alternative was UDF, 73% if the alternative was RPR -
a sizeable number in either case preferring the *majorité*. The
effect of this Socialist haemorrhage was serious. In 36 of the
50 constituencies 'carried' by François Mitterrand in 1974 which
the left needed to win and failed to win in 1978, the left had a
Communist candidate in the second ballot. Conversely of the 14
Giscard constituencies won by the left in 1978, 13 had Socialist
candidates in the second ballot. The diagram in Table 6.8 illus-
trates this handicap another way. With a Communist candidate

TABLE 6.8   PCF AND PS - RELATIVE PERFORMANCE, 2ND BALLOT

Constituencies (metropolitan)

| PCF top of left in first ballot | left score first bal- lot % | PS/MRG top of left in first ballot |

O Left in majority at 1st ballot. Left wins.

↓ Left in majority at 1st ballot. Left loses.

- Left in minority at 1st ballot. Left loses.

↗ Left in minority at 1st ballot. Left wins.

the left was losing in constituencies where it had had 54 or 56% in the first ballot. 16 Socialists but only 2 Communists managed, in seats where the left was in a minority at the first ballot, to generate that extra support to win. What is more this particular difficulty for the left has been growing (see Table 6.9). Where there has always been a Communist candidate in the second ballot, the second ballot losses have been getting worse.

Table 6.9   2nd ballot losses by Communists

Constituencies (78) where left's second ballot candidate is always Communist:-	1968	1973	1974
- Total left 1st ballot	47.8%	53.7%	55.9%
- PCF 2nd ballot	46.5%	51.8%	52.4%
- loss of support	-1.3	-1.9	-3.5

. A final indicator of the Communist handicap to the left can be found in an analysis of the left's average gain or loss from first ballot to second. (Table 6.10) It was a characteristic of the second ballot that all parties - *majorité* and opposition - tended to gain most second ballot votes where their side was weakest at the first and lose most votes where it was strongest.[4] In every type of constituency however the performance of the left was relatively better if it had a Socialist candidate.

One final point under the transfer of votes: where did the votes of the Ecologists and other unattached groups go? If one looks at some 50 constituencies where Ecologists did best (over 5½% at first ballot) - especially in Paris, Lower Normandy, Alsace, Rhône-Alps, and on the Mediterranean - one finds that these constituencies obey the laws demonstrated by Table 6.10. The left had the greatest gains where it is weakest and where the second ballot candidate is a Socialist: see Table 6.11.

TABLE 6.10   AVERAGE GAINS OR LOSSES BY LEFT AT SECOND BALLOT
(PERCENTAGE POINTS PER METROPOLITAN CONSTITUENCY)

	SCORE OF TOTAL LEFT AT FIRST BALLOT									
	OVER 55%		50% TO 55%		42% TO 49%		UNDER 42%		ALL	
SECOND BALLOT	No.	Left's Average Gain/Loss (% points)	No.	Left's Average Gain/Loss (% points)	No.	Left's Average Gain/Loss (% points)	No.	Left's Average Gain/Loss (% points)	No.	Left's Average Gain/Loss (% points)
Majorité represented by:-										
RPR	63	-3.7	61	-1.5	55	+0.5	36	+3.7	215	-0.8
UDF	46	-4.5	52	-1.3	64	+0.8	27	+3.3	189	-0.7
Opposition represented by:-										
PS/MRG	52	-2.3	68	-0.5	82	+1.4	58	+3.6	260	+1.65
PCF	57	-5.6	45	-2.7	37	-1.0	5	+2.6	144	-3.22
Second ballot duels:-										
RPR/PS or MRG	30	-1.9	35	-0.4	36	+1.1	33	+3.9	134	+0.7
RPR/PCF	33	-5.3	26	-2.9	19	-0.7	3	*	81	-3.2
UDF/PS or MRG	22	-2.8	33	-0.6	46	+1.7	25	+3.1	126	+0.6
UDF/PCF	24	-6.0	19	-2.5	18	-1.3	2	*	63	-3.2
All duels	109	-4.0	113	-1.38	119	+0.7	63	+3.5	404	-0.7

Table 6.11   ECOLOGISTS' VOTE - SECOND BALLOT
              (Ecologists' best constituencies)

	Ecol. (Average) 1st ballot	Left 2nd ballot (Average gain or loss)
Left weak - Socialist candidate (21)	8.3	+4.4
Left medium or strong - Socialist candidate (15)	6.5	+2.5
Communist candidate (11)	6.9	-0.5

These figures suggest - though of course they do not prove - that
a minority of Ecologists voted for the left at the second ballot
especially where the left was strong and that they seemed particularly reluctant to vote Communist. The strongest showing by
the Ecologists seems to have been made in areas where the left
is weak anyway: Manche, Bas-Rhin, Haut-Rhin.

It was an exciting second ballot. In 57 constituencies the
winner finished with less than 51% of the vote - including some
leaders of the *majorité* like Yves Guéna (RPR) or Jean-Jacques
Servan-Schreiber (UDF-Rad), [5] or Robert Boulin, Minister of
Labour. Some of the bright stars of the Socialist Party who had
won remarkable victories in 1973 were narrowly defeated: Charles
Josselin in Brittany, and Georges Frèche in Montpellier for
instance - the defeat of the latter being to a large extent attri-
butable to an abnormally large registration of French residents
overseas. Nationwide, the narrow lead of the *majorité* in second
ballot votes became a big Parliamentary victory in seats - a
familiar characteristic of 'winner takes all' simple majority
electoral systems.

It is very difficult for the left to win an election in
France. The diagram in Table 6.12 shows that 234 out of 491 seats
(only 12 short of an absolute majority) have never in recent history been out of the hands of the supporters of the present government. However in 1978 the *majorité* was actually able to win back
22 seats lost in 1973 and gained 6 new seats from the opposition.

TABLE 6.12   SAFE AND MARGINAL SEATS 1967-1978

	1967	1968	1973	1978	
_Majorité_* seats 1978 (Total 291)					
Continuously held by _majorité_ or Right**	————————————————————————————				234
(RPR)	————————————————————————————				(112)
(UDF/Centre)	————————————————————————————				(51)
(Alternating within _Maj._)	————————————————————————————				(71)
Discontinuous:	– – – – – ————————————————————				25
	– – – – – – – – – ————————————————				4
	– – – – – – – – – – – – ————————				11
	– – – – – ———————— – – – – ————				11

Opposition seats 1978 (Total 200)					
Continuously held by Opposition **	————————————————————————————				74
(PS/MRG)	————————————————————————————				(31)
(PCF)	————————————————————————————				(29)
(Alternating within Opp.)	————————————————————————————				(8)
Discontinuous:	———————— – – – – – ————————				51
	———————— – – – – – – – ————————				20
	———————————— – – – – – ————				5
	– – – – – – – – – – ————————————				26
	– – – – – – – – – – – – – – —————				25

(* includes former opposition Centrists now in _majorité_)
(** includes new constituencies created in 1973 and 1978)

The left continued to recover seats lost in the landslide of 1968 (51 in 1973, a further 20 in 1978). 26 seats won for the first time in 1973 were held in 1976 and 25 seats were won for the first time. It was not good enough.

The collapse of the credibility of a potential left-wing government was the principal component of the left's defeat and the aggressive style of the Communists changed too late in favour of unity for the left to have the dynamic current of success that in 1973 had gained it extra voters at the second ballot. The second ballot left the country, as at the 1974 Presidential election, divided exactly in two - 49.5 to 50.5. The unifiers - those that is to say associated with the consensus politics of Giscard d'Estaing and Mitterrand - did best in this election, though Mitterrand himself was gravely damaged by the collapse of his _Union de la Gauche_ strategy. The anti-consensus forces with the most aggressive style, RPR and PCF, came off worst - in terms of their capacity to mobilise the electors and their capacity to win extra second ballot votes.

NOTES

(1)   L'abstentionnisme electorale en France, Paris, FNSP, 1968, pp. 228-30.

(2)   This is not a uniquely anti-Communist phenomenon on the left. In Aude 2 for instance, where only the Socialist candidate Guidoni contested the second ballot, abstentions were up 7% and spoilt papers 22%.

(3)   J. Charlot (ed.) Quand la gauche va gagner, Paris, Moreau, 1973, p. 169.

(4)   In the 78 constituencies, considered in Table 6.9, where the left's second ballot candidate has always been Communist, the effect of this 'law' can be also seen:-

TABLE 6.13   Communist losses in relation to strength of left.

1st ballot	2nd ballot
1973-78 left - (10 cases)	PC + 1.2
1973-78 left steady (30 cases)	PC - 0.6
1973-78 left slightly + (15 cases)	PC - 1.4
1973-78 left strongly + (23 cases)	PC - 4.2

(5)   Jean-Jacques Servan-Schreiber's narrow win was invalidated by the Constitutional Council. At the subsequent by-election he lost.

CHAPTER 7. THE NEW PARLIAMENT

When the new National Assembly met for the first time in
early April the composition of the Parliamentary groups turned
out to be slightly different, on the *majorité* side especially,
from what the Ministry of the Interior's official classification
of the election results might have led one to suppose. The RPR
had gained six more members and the UDF had lost 14. Some, like
M. Frédéric-Dupont, elected as UDF, had changed parties. Some had
decided to sit in a group of unaffiliated '*non-inscrits*'.

TABLE 7.1   Parliamentary groups in the National Assembly.

PCF	86	(17.5% of Assembly)
PS*	113	(23.0%)
UDF	123	(25.0%)
RPR	154	(31.4%)
Non-inscrits	15	(3.1%)

* including 10 MRG of whom one (Robert Fabre) later
  joined the *non-inscrits*

The membership of the Assembly had undergone considerable
renewal at the elections. (Table 7.2)

TABLE 7.2   Parliamentary renewal

		% of new *députés**	
1958		72%	
1962		47%	
1967		33%	
1968		29%	
1973		36%	
1978		37%	
	- PS		43.4%
	- UDF		41.4%
	- PCF		40.7%
	- RPR		25.7%

* i.e. not members of preceding parliament

37% of *députés* had not been in the preceding Assembly and 33% had never been members at all. This rate of turnover is fairly high. Only the big electoral upheavals of 1958, when nearly all the Communists were defeated, and 1962 when nearly all non-Gaullist conservatives were, produce higher figures in the Fifth Republic.

The extent of this renewal in 1978 was the result of two factors. Firstly, a relatively high number of outgoing *députés* did not seek re-election. This was particularly so on the left with 18% of outgoing Communist members and 17% of Socialists and MRG retiring. In the case of the Communist Party, as we saw in Chapter 3, there was a deliberate policy by the leadership to bring new central committee members into the Parliamentary group by selecting them in safe Communist seats. Some Socialist *députés* were eliminated as candidates because their local constituency party sections declined to re-select them. This fate befell Jean Bastide, for example, in Gard 2 (a seat which the PS has now lost to the Communists). The other factor, of course, was actual defeat in the election. The competition within each alliance, as we saw in Chapter 6 (Table 6.2), contributed in no small measure.

As Table 7.2 shows, renewal of members in the Communist, Socialist, and UDF groups at over 40% was much higher than that which took place in the RPR. We have already noted that the principal strength of the RPR at the election was its high number of well-established *députés* seeking re-election. Three-quarters of its new Parliamentary group are therefore, not surprisingly, re-elected members of the old.

More new members means a younger Assembly (Table 7.3). 44% of members are now under 50 compared with 36% in 1973, and there are twice as many under-40's. The Socialist group is the youngest with an average age of 48. The average age of Communist and UDF members is 50, and that of the RPR group, with its predominance of re-elected *députés*, is over 53. One of the RPR's problems at future elections will be the ageing of its parliamentary elites and the electoral price it may have to pay for renewing them.

There are nineteen women in the new Assembly - 18 elected in March and the Socialist Edwige Avice who won a by-election in Paris a few months later. This feeble proportion, less than 4% of the total membership, which reflects the very low proportion of women candidates chosen by the parties (see 3.2), is at least some improvement on the preceding Assembly which had only 7 women members. The improvement, however, is exclusively the work of the Communist Party which systematically brought more women in as candidates in safe seats. The PCF has 12 women *députés* (14% of its group), the PS now 2 (2%), the UDF 3 (2%), and the RPR 2 (1%).

TABLE 7.3 Age-groups in the National Assembly.

	% of *députés*	
	1978	1973
Under 40	20.6	10.4
41-50	23.6	25.7
51-60	39.5	36.7
Over 60	16.3	27.2

Implantation locale - being a well-known mayor or councillor in one's constituency - is always, as we have seen, an important characteristic of French parliamentarians. It was particularly important in the 1978 election. We noted in Chapter 5 (Table 5. how local 'notability' was the main explanatory variable in explaining which were the more successful candidates of the *majorité* in different constituencies. In the new Assembly 83% of *députés* are local councillors or mayors (see Table 7.4). The figure in the Socialist group is no less than 94% reflecting both French Socialist tradition and the big Socialist gains in local elections in 1976 and 1977.

The background of members, in terms of occupation, is very much in keeping with the Fifth Republic's traditions - very few working-class members, a large number from the professions and teaching (see Table 7.5). Within the groups, however, there are variations to this general theme. In the Communist group former manual and clerical workers (mainly permanent party officials before their election to the Assembly) constitute 52% of the members. The Socialist group is dominated by the teaching profession which contributes four members out of 10: the *'République des Professeurs'* is not dead! The other professions too, and business

TABLE 7.4 *Députés* as local councillors[2]

	National Assembly	PC	PS	UDF	RPR
Members of					
- Municipal council and *conseil général*	46%	34%	59%	45%	44%
- *Conseil général* only	15%	20%	9%	10%	18%
- Municipal council only	22%	29%	26%	21%	19%
- No local mandate	17%	17%	6%	24%	19%

TABLE 7.5 *Députés* - professional background[2]

	National Assembly	PC	PS	UDF	RPR
Professions	19%	2%	13%	28%	24%
Teaching	18%	25%	44%	8%	8%
- Secondary and Higher	14%	12%	35%		
- Primary	4%	13%	9%		
Higher civil service	12%	-	8%	16%	17%
Middle management	12%	13%	16%	10%	10%
Senior management	10%	1%	7%	13%	15%
Industrialists and employers	10%	-	7%	15%	13%
Manual workers	7%	38%*	-	-	-
Farmers	4%	5%	1%	5%	4%
Clerical workers	3%	14%*	1%	-	-
Engineers	2%	-	3%	2%	4%
Shopkeepers and self-employed	2%	1%	-	2%	3%
Other	1%	1%	-	1%	1%

* most Communist candidates continue to list their original occupations but many in fact have long been permanent party officials.

management, are well represented in the Socialist group. In pre-vious Parliaments (we have no data for the new one) an analysis of the parents and grandparents of Socialist members in high-status occupations reveals origins somewhat more humble than those of *députés* from similar professions in the *majorité*[3].

In the *majorité* there is a striking similarity in profes-sional background of members of the 'liberal professions', top civil servants (of whom, by the way, about half are graduates of ENA - the prestigious National School of Administration), and com-pany directors. When we looked at the sociology of the electorate we found four main political parties but only three electorates. In Parliament it is just the same - four parliamentary groups in party terms, but only three by professional background.

Roland Cayrol and the other authors of le député français[4] have pointed to the three routes to membership of the National Assembly: the route which begins with entry into politics as a humble party activist, the route which starts with membership of a local council, and finally the route that starts in a minister's *cabinet*. The authors point out how it is the third route which has become more and more characteristic of the Fifth Republic. The *cursus honorum* to political power, today, is less likely to be the classic one of municipal council, mayoralty, *conseil général*, *député*, minister. It is very frequently ENA, one of the *Grands Corps* of the public service such as the Inspectorate of Finance, membership of a *cabinet* or the personal entourage of a minister, then *député* and minister. Sometimes being a minister precedes being a *député* as in the case of ministers taken straight from the public service like Maurice Couve de Murville or René Haby, and of course many ministers,such as President Giscard d'Estaing's first two Foreign Secretaries Jean Sauvagnargues and Louis de Guiringaud, are never Members of Parliament at all. The ministerial *cabinet* is where the dividing line between administration and politics is at its most blurred and it is through the ministerial *cabinet* that many ENA-trained administrators, like Jacques Chirac for instance, pass to their political careers.

The three routes to membership of the National Assembly were all well-travelled in 1978 but it is significant that of the

28 new *députés* of the *majorité* aged under 40, 10 were straight
from ministerial *cabinets*. Five are RPR: Michel Barnier, at 27
the youngest member of the Assembly, J-P Bechter, a protégé of
Chirac and now *député* for the next constituency to Chirac in the
Corrèze where he had also been in the local Préfet's *cabinet*,
J-P Delalande, J. Godfrain former member of the Elysée staff, and
P. Seguin from Raymond Barre's *cabinet*. Five others are UDF:
J. Douffiagues, G. Longuet and A. Madelin - all three combining
important roles in the organisation of the *Giscardien* Republican
Party with their *cabinet* posts - D. Mariani and J-P Pierre-Bloch.
Several of these new *députés* are former students of ENA as are
some of the newly-elected younger Socialists such as Laurent Fabius,
an economic adviser to François Mitterrand, and Alain Richard who
had the distinction of defeating Michel Poniatowski, former Minister of the Interior, in the election.

There are also plenty of new *députés* who have followed the
more classic route to the Assembly. A Socialist like Alain
Chenard, Mayor of Nantes, is a good example of the local notable
turned *député*. There are plenty of party activists too who have
graduated to become members of the Assembly. This is still the
principal Communist road to Parliament. Nearly all the newly-
elected younger Communists hold some party office at local or national level: Myriam Barbera, a hairdresser in Sète, is a member of
the local federal Secretariat, Renê Visse is the Secretary of the
Ardennes Federation, Claude Wargnies a party member for 20 years
and federal bureau member in the Nord. This route to Parliament
is not confined only to the left: Michel Noir, a new RPR *député* in
Lyon,has been a Gaullist activist and party office-holder at local
level since the mid-1960's. Party activists such as these accede
generally to local councils before becoming *députés* - indeed all
those we have just referred to are councillors. Perhaps the most
classic example of a new young member graduating from militant to
notable to *député* is Dominique Taddéi, the 39 year-old university
professor, Socialist party member for 20 years, a member of the
party's *comité directeur* since 1969, of its executive bureau since
1971, inheritor of the old Socialist mayoralty of Avignon in 1977,

député for that city in 1978, and perhaps a *ministrable* if the left had won the election.

NOTES

(1) See Roland Cayrol, Jean-Luc Parodi, Colette Ysmal Le député français, Paris, Presses de la Fondation Nationale des Sciences Politiques, 1973.

(2) Tables 7.4 and 7.5 are derived from Alain Guedé and Gilles Fabre-Rosane 'Portrait robot du député 1978', Le Matin, 19 avril 1978.

(3) Le député français, ibid. p. 48.

(4) ibid. pp. 119-20.

CHAPTER 8. IF THE LEFT HAD WON

'If only the left had won', a rather conservative American political scientist complained at a recent conference. 'Then we could have seen whether the constitution worked, whether the civil service or the army would have remained loyal to the legal government, and whether the Communist Party would have behaved itself!'. It would be intriguing to know the details of contingency plans prepared by NATO, by the French defence and security forces, by finance and industry on the assumption that a victory by the left would be a giant step towards Communist aims of assisting world-domination by the Soviet Union. But just how radical would a coalition government of the left have been? In all democracies the need to maintain public support and to cope with external realities like inflation or the balance of payments make the full implementation of party programmes - whether of the left or the right-.impossible. New governments soon find themselves reminding their supporters that Rome was not built in a day.

The prospect of electoral victory by a left which included a large Communist Party with a Stalinist past aroused misgivings in four areas: the economy, the constitution, liberties, and foreign affairs. President Giscard d'Estaing was right, in our view, to point to the first of these as the area in which fears were the most justifiable. The credibility of the *programme commun* was seriously jeopardised by the conflict between Socialists and Communists, the competitive bidding of electoral promises between them, and the obvious lack of a working relationship on economic and social questions that was revealed. But of course it was largely because of this conflict that the left lost the election. If the PCF had been in a mood to help the left to win the election, it would not have been in a mood to make aggressive and unrealistic demands for sudden and extreme change. The actual economic policies of a Socialist-Communist coalition cannot really be deduced from the auction that took place, in September 1977 and after, over nationalisation and the minimum wage. However moderate or otherwise, though, the economic intentions of an incoming

government might have been, there could still have been the problem of the flight of capital and a self-fulfilling prophecy about
a collapse of confidence in the currency.

Anxieties about constitutional difficulties centred round
the fact that there has never yet been in the twenty years of the
Fifth Republic a case of opposition between the President of the
Republic and a newly-elected Parliamentary majority. President
Giscard d'Estaing, however, firmly ruled out his own resignation[1]
and never even hinted in his speeches at a constitutional or
regime crisis if the left won the election. A summary of the range
of options open to the President is presented in the notes at the
end of this chapter.[2]

Had the left won, the President would have had to approve
laws voted by Parliament which he might not have cared for in some
cases. However, using his constitutional power, he could have
withheld his signature from non-legislative decrees and regula-
tions, have blocked undesirable nominations to senior posts in the
public service such as ambassadors, *préfets*, senior officials in
administration or education. The constitution also gives him the
right to address messages to Parliament, and of course he could
have given interviews or press conferences. He would therefore
have been able to moderate and restrain his government and to express in a spectacular way any reservations he felt about what it
was trying to do. Finally he would have retained the power to
dissolve Parliament and call for new elections if he felt the
public was ready to throw the government out. All of this demonstrates that for the opposition really to win power in France, it
must win a Presidential election.

On the loyalty of army and civil service to a new government,
most informed commentators, mindful of the discreet high-level con-
tacts that were being established with Socialist leaders, believe
that this would not have presented any great difficulty. No doubt
there would have been prefectoral and other changes. No doubt there
would have been opposition within ministries to some policies.
For instance, one wonders how the officials of DOM-TOM Ministry
(Overseas Departments and Territories) would have reacted to the
programme commun policy of recognising the right to self-determination of all the areas they administered - instead of 'Vive le

Québec libre!', 'Vive la Martinique libre!'. On balance, however, it is our view that there was no reason to expect a constitutional crisis, a collapse of presidential authority, or an unconstitutional revolt within the public service to have followed a victory by the left at the polls.

Foreign and defence policy under a possible coalition of the left caused some of the deepest anxieties, arising, naturally enough, from the long devotion to the Soviet Union by the French Communist Party - a devotion only slightly scaled down by criticisms of Soviet persecution which have been a careful but developint theme of PCF pronouncements during recent years. However the assumption that a coalition government in France with even 50% Communist participation would inevitably be a Quisling regime bent on betraying the country to the Soviet Union seems to us a trifle hasty. In the first place it was extremely improbable that the PCF would have been able successfully to insist on the portfolio either of Foreign Affairs or Defence[3]. Secondly there is contingency planning in Western defence circles to cope with the eventuality of Communist participation in a Western government - be it Iceland, Italy, Portugal or France. Thirdly there is evidence, in Soviet coolness towards Mitterrand, in the rather ostentatious support given to Giscard d'Estaing by the Soviet Embassy in the 1974 Presidential election, in the Soviet approval for the foreign policy of de Gaulle and Pompidou, that the Soviet Union, like any other rather conservative great power, prefers the *status quo* to 'destabilisation' in Europe. Indeed some have seen the electorally suicidal behaviour of the PCF in 1977-78 as reflecting Soviet preference for the *majorité* to win the election! Fourthly the foreign and defence policy of the *programme commun* is remarkably similar to the policies of the present government. 'Respecting France's present alliances', a government of the left would operate 'a policy independent of military blocs'. It would pursue mutual and balanced force reductions, it would maintain (the PCF was the initiator of this change of policy) France's independent nuclear deterrent. It would respect 'the rights of existence and sovereignty of all the states' in the Middle East, 'notably of the state of Israel as well as the national rights of the Arab people of Palestine'. It would maintain national freedom of action within the EEC. In short, apart from nebulous and unrealisable aims like demanding 'the simultaneous dissolution of both NATO and the Warsaw Pact', it is a foreign policy much like that of present government.

This consensus between government and opposition in foreign policy is one of the themes in the declarations of President Giscard d'Estaing dealing with the need for 'reasonable cohabitation' between political adversaries. In most democracies, indeed in France, there is broad agreement over fundamentals like national security and national interests overseas. The President would like to have regular meetings with opposition leaders over such matters of over-riding national importance. The trouble is that, although there appear to be no serious differences between government and opposition on the fundamental issues of defence and foreign policy, any such consultation is regarded, especially by the Communist leaders but also by Socialists, as 'class collaboration'. Reason says that there is no necessity for conflict - 'war will not take place' - but there is conflict just the same.

There was some conflict over foreign affairs during the election campaign but it was not over the substance of foreign policy but over who should direct it. If there had been a government of the left the Prime Minister, as Mitterrand declared in his speeches, would have expected a major role in the orientation of French foreign policy. However, President Giscard d'Estaing, as he made clear in his speeches, remains attached to the notion that the French Head of State should be the principal *interlocuteur* and initiator of foreign policy. The constitutional rather than the policy issues here might well have proved to be the principal source of difference between the two men had another 1% of the population willed them to work together.

The final element of mistrust, very widely felt by Socialists as well as supporters of the government, concerns Communist attachment to liberal democracy and its freedoms. The leadership of the Communist Party does not exactly inspire confidence. Democratic centralism, the denunciation of dissidents, the perpetual unanimity, the Stalinist jargon, the refusal to admit error, the

admiration for the Soviet system of government - all these and
many other aspects of Communist organisation, beliefs, and style
convey a strong impression that the PCF and liberal democracy are
strangers. Let us assume for the sake of argument that the leaders of the French Communist Party do in fact, with ruthless and
unwavering resolve, want their country to become a Soviet-style
dictatorship,and ask ourselves if a victory by the left at the
polls in March 1978 would have helped the fulfilment of that aim.
How does one actually set about the task of setting up a totalitarian police state in a country that is used to freedom - particularly where there are no apocalyptic economic problems like
hyper-inflation or mass unemployment, no widespread poverty or
oppression? How does one, particularly as the junior partner in
a coalition, set about dismantling a constitution that guarantees
free elections and suppressing opposition and the freedom of information? Democracy, once it has taken hold in good soil, is a much
sturdier plant than is supposed by some of its defenders. If
Georges Marchais had become Minister of the Interior, how would he
have used his powers over the police, the *préfets*, and over local
administration to make France more Communist? Apart from the ac-
quisition of some inside knowledge of the security services and
the promotion of some pro-Communists (removeable at the next ministerial reshuffle), there is not very much practical action that
can be taken. If he or his colleagues had seemed bent on the
unconstitutional, the illegal or the subversive, they would pre-
sumably have been dismissed from office as in 1947 - either directly
by the Prime Minister as the constitution lays down or by the formation of a new government on the initiative of the President of
the Republic. The Communist Party does not have enough support
in the country for its dismissal from office in such circumstances
to be the cause of a grave governmental crisis. The role of the
PCF in a coalition government would probably have been like that
of the left-wing Tribune Group in relation to a Labour Government
in Great Britain. It would have attacked the Socialist Party
leadership for being too kind to capitalism, it would have demanded
more nationalisation, it would have wanted more protection and an
increased role for unions in industry and consultation with

government, it would have wanted taxation to be directed more towards wealth and privilege, and it would have wanted to be seen as leading the field in demanding increased welfare spending. Much of that would have been irresponsible, demagogic, and anti-libertarian - but it would not have made France a Communist dictatorship.

Above all the experience of a coalition government of the left would be likely to have been very short. At the first major disagreement, economic downturn, unpopularity or public disillusion, the President of the Republic could have called for new elections. The price of freedom is eternal vigilance. That is true but it should not be an excuse for prejudiced and intolerant judgement. Once again, it seems to us, good sense could, like Hector, have decreed 'war will not take place'.

NOTES

(1) A SOFRES opinion poll (February 1977) found that 60% of people (including 51% of Socialist supporters) wanted him to stay if the left won.

(2) Presidential options

For a President of the Republic who finds himself confronted with a Parliamentary majority that does not support him, the following options are available:

Dissolution of Parliament

- useful for a newly-elected President who has no Parliamentary majority to support his policies. A new Parliamentary election could well produce one.

- a dangerous strategy for a President facing a newly-elected Parliamentary majority which opposed him

    (a) a new victory for the new majority would be a vehement disavowal of the President

    (b) the power to dissolve Parliament cannot be used twice within a 12 month period (Art. 12 of constitution).

Resignation of President

- threat of Presidential resignation if Parliamentary election returns a majority unfavourable to him is a powerful but dangerous electoral weapon

- if re-elected, authority reinforced

- if defeated, new alignment of Presidency and Parliamentary majority.

Referendum on powers of President

- constitution requires that referenda be proposed by government (Art. 11 of constitution), so there would need to be a government willing to make the proposition, and any modification of the constitution should, strictly speaking, be passed by Parliament first (Art. 89 - a procedure not followed in 1962 and 1969)

- defeat of referendum would force Presidential resignation.

Postponement of any further electoral consultation

- requires the appointment of a government that will have the support of new Parliamentary majority. (Composition and leadership of government will depend on such factors as cohesiveness of new majority coalition)

- the constitutional prerogatives of the Prime Minister, especially those where the President needs his agreement, would be of more importance than so far in the Fifth Republic :-

Respective powers of President and Prime Minister:

President - appointment of Prime Minister (Art. 8)

      - dissolution of National Assembly (Art. 12)

      - exercise of exceptional powers (Art. 16)

      - right to address Parliament by message (Art.18)

      - power to invoke Constitutional Council either for unconstitutional character of laws or of clauses in a treaty (Art. 61)

      - nomination of 3 members (including Chairman) of Constitutional Council (Art. 56)

      - decision not to submit a Constitutional law to referendum (Art. 11)

Prime Minister and Government

      - fixing Parliamentary agenda (Art. 48)

      - power to resolve procedural deadlocks in Parliament (Art. 45)

Powers needing agreement of President and Prime Minister

      - calling meetings of Council of Ministers (Art. 19)

      - requiring Parliament to reconsider a Bill (Art. 10)

      - recourse to referendum (Art. 11)

      - signature of regulations and decrees decided at Council of Ministers (Art. 19)

      - appointment to top civil and military posts (Art. 19)

      - proposals to revise constitution (Art. 89)

      - calling of special sessions of Parliament (Art. 29)

- politically the most advantageous option for the President:

    - he retains sufficient powers to moderate government action

    - he can choose most favourable moment for dissolution and new elections.

(see Jean-Luc Parodi, 'le cas français: les données d'un conflit éventuel entre le Président de la République et la majorité parlementaire issue des nouvelles élections législatives', France-Forum, avril-mai 1977, pp. 23-34).

(3) 51% of people, according to an opinion poll by Démoscopie
(Feb 1978) were in favour of there being Communist ministers
if the left won the election (37% against). The ministerial
offices they thought Communists should fill were:-

TABLE 8.1   Opinions on Ministries for Communists

	Communist as Minister % in favour
Labour, Social Affairs	56*
Health	42*
Industry	36
Agriculture	32
Justice	32
Economy and Finance	27
Education	25
Interior	23**
Defence	22**
Foreign Affairs	17**

 * cases where those in favour outnumbered those against.
** a majority of Socialist voters were opposed to Communist
   appointments to these three ministries.

(Source: Publimétrie, Feb. 1978)

CHAPTER 9. AFTER THE ELECTION

The left, of course, did not win. It lost because the
Communist Party judged that it was less important to win the election than to avoid being eclipsed by the Socialist Party. It lost
because, largely as a result of the tactical preoccupations of the
Communist leadership, it could not provide a guarantee of credible
alternative government that respected democratic fundamentals.

Rivalry between partners in both coalitions - *majorité* as
well as left - was one of the principal themes of the election.
It was suicidal in the case of the left in March 1978 just as, to
a lesser extent and in a less important contest, it had been for
the *majorité* in the municipal elections of March 1977. The aggressive tone of the PCF as it responded to the danger of electoral
extinction by its Socialist partners is not very different to that
of the RPR as it faced the identical threat from the *Giscardiens*.
In both cases an aggressive campaign against its partner permitted
each party to regain control of its own electorate and its own
strongholds. However in both alliances the more moderate party,
the *Giscardien* UDF on the one hand, the PS on the other, showed
the greater attractiveness to the electorate at large, as our analysis of the second ballot showed in particular. The outcome of
the election was a source of great satisfaction for President
Giscard d'Estaing. With renewed authority and prestige he recon-
structed his government and set about the task of reconciliation.

a. The President's victory.

In the period immediately following the election, relief
about the result seemed to outweigh disappointment (see Table 9.1).
Those who had voted for the left generally expressed disappointment but opinion surveys reveal that one Socialist voter in five
declared himself 'satisfied' with the outcome.

This general feeling of relief, the re-assurance that 'war
will not take place', was combined with an admirably democratic
acceptance of the verdict of universal suffrage. Despite the apocalyptic predictions of some leaders of the left, there was no

movement of social discontent, no strife, no upheaval in the
period following the elections. The feeling that it was the end
of a long and continuous campaign, through which people had lived
for over two years, no doubt contributed to this general acceptance of the outcome.

TABLE 9.1   Public Opinion and the Election Results

Question: 'Are you on the whole satisfied or disappointed by the
          election results?'

	1978	1974 Presidential election
Satisfied	51%	46%
Disappointed	35%	40%
No opinion	14%	14%

(Source: SOFRES)

With the parties of the left stunned and paralysed by their
defeat, it was to those confirmed in power, to the President of
the Republic especially, but also to the new Parliamentary majority,
that words and actions first returned. The *majorité*, once more
safe from defeat, the enemy chased from the field, quickly returned to its own rivalries and divisions. The election of President
of the National Assembly - the 'Speaker' of the French Parliament -
provided an opportunity for conflict.

The battle for the *'perchoir'* between Jacques Chaban-Delmas
and Edgar Faure, the outgoing President, contained many intriguing
elements of paradox. Firstly the UDF presented no candidate of
its own but supported a Gaullist of true orthodox hue while the
RPR supported Faure, an affiliated member of the RPR group (*'appar-
enté'*) who had also recently tried to become President of the
Radical Party! Secondly, the candidate supported by the *Giscardiens* was none other than the opponent of Giscard d'Estaing in the
1974 presidential elections. Finally Jacques Chirac, who, in 1974,
had abandoned Chaban-Delmas for Giscard d'Estaing and thereby contributed to the latter's victory, found himself in 1978 opposed to
both. The terrain was unfavourable for Chirac because a secret

ballot election makes furtive breaches of discipline only too easy. Chaban-Delmas won because a number of Gaullists defied their new leader and voted for their old *'compagnon'* at the first ballot. (Table 9.2).

TABLE 9.2   Election of President of the National Assembly.

	1st ballot	2nd ballot
J. Chaban-Delmas	153	276
E. Faure	136	Withdrew
P. Mauroy (PS)	112	112
M. Andrieux (PCF)	86	85
Abstentions and blank ballots	4	17

Indirectly the winner in this battle with Chirac, unchallenged figurehead of a new presidential party, President Giscard d'Estaing appeared in the post-electional period as the real victor in the field. His rating in the opinion polls (59% satisfied, 30% dissatisfied) reached its highest figure for three years. If there had been a Presidential election he would, according to the polls, have defeated Mitterrand 60-40. It was the ideal moment to perfect his presidential image by offering yesterday's adversaries terms for 'reasonable cohabitation', by inviting political and union leaders to meet him, and even, a few months later (and incidentally thereby driving another nail into the coffin of the *union de la gauche*), proposing that Robert Fabre, ex-leader of the MRG, should head an enquiry with rather vague terms of reference into the subject of employment.

The President has always made it clear in the language he employs on the occasion of government reshuffles that he personally decides on the composition of the government team. The government he appointed after the election was a Presidential government. Like the preceding one, it was headed by Raymond Barre, and it maintained the same general balance between UDF and RPR: three-quarters UDF (including the non-parliamentary ministers taken from the public service), one-quarter RPR. Furthermore it is noticeable that the RPR ministers like Peyrefitte or Galley, belong to the Chaban-Delmas rather than to the Chirac camp.

b. Politics in the Autumn.

Six months later the political landscape looked rather
different and one had the impression of having been transported
several years back in time. After its April peak, the rating of
the President began to decline and the Prime Minister, probably as
a result of persistent unemployment and inflation augmented by the
post-electoral economic measures relaxing price controls, beat
his own personal record for unpopularity: in September 31% satisfied, 58% dissatisfied.

The first opinion polls testing voting intentions at a new
election recorded this discontent and once again it was the Socialist Party that seemed to be its sole beneficiary. (Table 9.3).

TABLE 9.3   Voting intentions six months after the elections.

PSU, Extreme-left	3%	)	
PCF	18%	)	53%
PS/MRG	32%	)	
Ecologists	3%		
UDF	21%	)	
RPR	20%	)	44%
Other *majorité*	3%	)	

(figures exclude 'don't knows' etc: 21% of sample)

(Source: SOFRES - Nouvel Observateur, 25-27 September, 1978)

More importantly, in the five by-elections which took place
the left swept the board. The Constitutional Council, which has
the job of considering the numerous complaints about the regularity of election results, declared invalidated five of the closest
March results. Thus 2 Socialist *députés*, a Communist, a UDF, and
a RPR had to fight by-elections. The *députés* of the left were all
re-elected. Those of the *majorité*, however, including Jean-
Jacques Servan-Schreiber, the leader of the Radical Party who had
held his seat by 22 votes in March, who was much disliked by the
RPR, and who had used pictures of himself with President Giscard
d'Estaing as his by-election posters, were heavily defeated by
their Socialist opponents. Incidentally this was the first time
in the Fifth Republic that a *député* invalidated by the Constitutional Council was not re-elected.[1] All results, just like those

in the period 1973-1976, confirmed the decline of both *majorité* and PCF and tremendous gains for the Socialists. Of course, these were not elections at which the country's future was going to be decided - confirming the trend of the 1970's whereby the electorate always vote for the left except when the left might win power. Voting turnout is lower in by-elections, and the by-election gains of the previous parliament did not on the whole stand up at the general election in March. Too much significance must therefore not be read into these results. (Table 9.4 and, for comparison with past by-elections, Table 1.3).

TABLE 9.4   By-elections - Summer 1978

(% change from March 1978)

	Absten- tions	PC	1st ballot PS	Total left (inc. ext. left)	2nd ballot (addition- al gains)
Seine St. Denis 9 (PCF)	+37.2	*	*	-3.1	+0.8
Gers 1 (PS)	+ 5	*	*	+4.2	no second ballot
Pas de Calais 4 (PS)	+ 8.6	-6.8	+17.3	+6.0	+6.3
Meurthe-et- Moselle 1 (UDF)	+22.6	-4.6	+11.5	+5.1	+4.6**
Paris 16 (RPR)	+24.3	-1.3	+10.7	+6.9	+0.5**

* no Socialist candidate against PCF *député* in Seine St. Denis, no Communist candidate against the PS in the Gers

** seats gained by Socialists

There are other indications that the great pre-electoral popularity of the Socialist Party has been recovered. A SOFRES poll conducted in late September and published in the Figaro showed that 54% of people had a good opinion of the PS against 32% who had an unfavourable one. Figures for the other parties (RPR 37 and 44, UDF 34 and 38, MRG 33 and 40, PCF 27 and 57) show that the PS is the only party to enjoy a favourable rating. The proportion of people having a good opinion of the UDF was down 10 points from March - reflecting more the collapse of the Prime

Minister's rating rather than the more gentle decline of the
President's. The 'aggressive' parties RPR and PCF were the most
positively disliked, the PCF no doubt continuing to reap the harvest of its anti-Socialist campaign. Most political leaders saw
their opinion poll ratings fall in this period. Paradoxically it
was the Socialist leader François Mitterrand who was the most
affected (-15 points since before the election according to IFOP)
at the very moment when his party was on the way up in polls and
by-elections. It was without doubt his image as the symbol of
unity, leader of the *union de la gauche*, which had received severe
damage in a period of continuing disunity. Other important political leaders to be liked less than Mitterrand and disliked more
included Jacques Chirac (43% good opinion, 40% bad opinion) and
Georges Marchais (32 and 51).

There seemed to be an extraordinary immobility in French
politics. For the seventh time since its first serious attempt
at union in the Presidential election of 1965, the left had lost
the battle to win power - its defeat being caused not by gerry-
mandering, nor by all the overseas seats belonging to the *majorité*,
nor by the television, but by its own divisions. The left seems
to do best when it is represented by a single Socialist candidate,
as in the Presidential elections of 1965 and 1974, by joint lists
of candidates, in which the Communists appear in less sharp relief
(for example, in the municipal elections of 1977), or by an alliance in which the PS appears as the rising partner. Conversely
the left is least likely to win when the salience or 'visibility'
of the PCF is greatest, especially when it gives its allies an
even more ferocious treatment than its adversaries might reasonably expect.

Beaten in its expectation of power, in retreat from its
successes at the local elections in 1976 and 1977, and, very
slightly, from the second ballot of the Presidential election in
1974, the left nonetheless had its most successful parliamentary
election in the Fifth Republic. The balance of political forces
in France is such as to allow no change of strategy and no breaking of ranks. The dialectic of the two blocs, the ongoing insti-
tutional and electoral systems, and the political calendar compel

all the main political groups to continue with the same strategies and the same alliances, altering only their *modus operandi*. The double contest of 1978, however, the contest between opposition and *majorité* and the rivalry within each alliance, could not fail to have left scars.

On the left the PCF is still paying the cost of 1977. The debate which opened within the party and which the leadership clearly cannot control is one of the most fundamental it has ever undergone. Its gradual move, during the past 10 years or so, away from the Stalinist model, gives the party more problems than it resolves. Every step along the road emphasises either its responsibility for the past or invites criticisms for the steps it has not yet made. Relatively authoritarian in the manner of its relative destalinisation, the PC is caught in something of a trap. How does it illustrate its liberalisation without tolerating opposition groups within its ranks? How does it maintain its nature and identity as a Communist Party without cracking down on such opposition? Throughout the summer of 1978 hardly a week passed without a virulent article in le Monde by Jean Elleinstein, a leading Communist Party intellectual, attacking the party leadership for failing to understand contemporary economic reality in a country where the working class is not facing the impoverishment foreseen by Marx, for failing to disassociate itself utterly from the imperialist foreign policy and the anti-libertarian bureaucratic state machine of the Soviet Union. There have even been manifestoes signed by hundreds of Party members condemning the Party for breaking the union of the left. All these actions have been condemned repreatedly in the columns of the Party press and in speeches by leaders but, up to the time of writing, there have been no expulsions and Elleinstein remains director of the Party's *Centre d'étude et de recherche Marxistes*. Whatever the outcome of all these disagreements, it is the internal workings of Party democracy which are in question, and quite clearly, the means, Stalinist or liberal, by which the Party leadership puts an end to this *contestation* will have an important effect on the way French political life as a whole will develop in the days to come.

Getting the CGT to take a strongly pro-Communist line in the argument with the Socialists is another aspect of the PCF's election campaign which could have important consequences. This emphasis on the close links between France's largest union organisation and the Communist Party will not help to stop the decline in support for the CGT amongst non-unionised workers - an important point in a country where actual union membership is very low - and it will make relations with the other big union, the CFDT, even more difficult.

The Socialist Party is frequently urged to change its strategy because of the difficulties of having the PCF as an ally. However, the bi-polar government-opposition system that has emerged in the Fifth Republic, the constraints of the electoral system, and, in particular perhaps, the nature of the competition on the left all prevent such a change. It has been its firm identification with the left, of which the alliance with the PCF has been the most visible and tangible sign, that has made it possible for the PS to lift Socialist support from the 12-15% of the early days of the Fifth Republic, when the Party was still associated with Fourth Republic centrism, to the 25% it has today. It has also been possible to hold Communist support down to the 20% level at which it has been blocked since 1958. Thus the Party continues to govern in coalition with the Communists the towns and cities won by their joint lists in 1977, but is at the same time seeking a less rigid and programmatic form of alliance. The electoral calendar for 1979 is favourable from the point of view of this type of development. The elections for *conseils généraux* require an alliance for the second ballot but impose no commitments to a programme *commun*, or other. The European Parliament election is on the basis of proportional representation with each party presenting national lists and in this case there is no need for an alliance at all and an admirable opportunity is provided for an experiment in independence.

It is therefore less in terms of strategy than in terms of leadership that the question of 'renewal' first made itself felt. In particular, the succession to the mantle of François Mitterrand, twice presidential candidate, first Secretary of the Party since its relaunching in 1971, symbol of *union de la gauche* since 1965, is open, and public opinion seems already to have designated the next leader of the Party. (Table 9.5).

TABLE 9.5 Future Socialist leadership

Question: If François Mitterrand retired as Socialist Party leader, who would you wish to see succeed him?

Michel Rocard	23%	(39% of Socialist voters)
Pierre Mauroy	15%	(19%)
Jean-Pierre Chevènement (leader of left-wing CERES group)	9%	(9%)
Gaston Defferre	8%	(6%)
No opinion	39%	(27%)

(IFOP opinion poll, le Point, 24-29 août 1978)

On the right, the same constraints of a bi-polar political system and two-ballot electoral system impede any aspirations to independence that any parties might have. Propelled by Jacques Chirac, the RPR continues to become more like the RPF, the aggressively nationalist and anti-Communist Gaullist movement of the late 1940's and early 1950's. However the gap between the movement, which is entirely under the control of the party machine and its leader, and the less cohesive RPR parliamentary group, most of whose members were elected more on the basis of *majorité* union than partisan differences, threatens to grow wider. In addition the Fifth Republic constitution limits the range of Parliamentary action and if there arises any disagreement between the RPR and the government which negotiation cannot resolve, the government, by making legislative issues a matter of confidence, has the power to make unruly *députés* choose between supporting the government and facing the voters again. How many RPR *députés* would be willing in the final analysis to support a motion of censure against the government? How many of those who did so would be sure of holding their seats in the ensuing election? Merely to pose the question is to show how limited is the RPR's freedom of action.

The 1981 Presidential election is already looming on the political horizon. As far as the *majorité* is concerned, the candidature of President Giscard d'Estaing seems virtually certain and the only doubt hovers over whether Chirac will stand or not. On the left, the PCF has already announced that, unlike in 1965 and 1974, it will this time present a candidate and it will be intriguing to see who that candidate will be. Whether the Socialist candidate for the Presidency will be Mitterrand again, over 65 in 1981, or a successor is another interesting question. Opinion polls in the Autumn of 1978 suggested that Rocard would do just as well. (Table 9.6).

TABLE 9.6   Presidential election possibilities

	1st ballot	2nd ballot
Marchais	17%	-
Mitterrand	31%	47%
Giscard d'Estaing	36%	53%
Chirac	16%	-
(figures exclude don't knows - 16% and 17%)		
Marchais	18%	-
Rocard	30%	47%
Giscard d'Estaing	36%	53%
Chirac	16%	-
(figures exclude don't knows - 15% and 17%)		

(SOFRES)

It seems likely therefore that the first ballot of the Presidential election will reproduce three years later the same four-cornered contest as 1978. At the second ballot, however, it will be the representatives of the moderate wing of each big alliance who will face each other. In France, as in most stable Western democracies, electoral competition is increasingly centrist and increasingly dominated by moderates.

c. Democracy and the alternation of power

        The 1978 election solved nothing. The problems it posed
remain problems for the country. No legitimate democracy can be
esteemed such unless the peaceful alternation of power from government to opposition occurs. The principal blockage at the moment
- the existence of the PCF - is not of the government's making.
However the consequence has been that the same men have been in
power for almost a quarter of a century. This ruling elite, seem-
ingly immune from censure by the electorate, is protected too, by
the rigid application of a constitution designed to curb irresponsible parliamentary behaviour, from parliamentary scrutiny of the
use and abuse of executive power. The opposition and its supporters are totally excluded from any share in responsibility and
consequently safe from the requirement to behave responsibly. Any
attempt by the President of the Republic to bring opposition leaders into some kind of normal relationship with the executive have
been rebuffed - either by his own *majorité*, especially the RPR,
who refuse to give up their own monopoly of access to privilege
and patronage, or by the opposition, especially the Communists,
who see any cooperation as 'class collaboration' or implying approval for the actions of the executive. One of the main themes of
the Giscard d'Estaing presidency has been the search for *décris-
pation*: the removal of tension and perpetual hostility between
political elites of government and opposition, so that the normal
harmonious functioning of a democratic system can be assured. In
his post-electoral broadcast of March 22nd he declared that the
problem in France was not that she is electorally 'cut in two'.
Such division was perfectly normal. 'What is regrettable is the
state of relationships between majority and opposition'. He called
for 'reasonable cohabitation'. In the period that followed the
election some small steps, noted earlier, were taken: the Presidential meetings with Mitterrand and Marchais, the inclusion of
some Socialists in the Presidential delegation to the United
Nations in the summer of 1978, the appointment of Robert Fabre,
who had resigned as leader of the Left-Radicals after the elections, to lead a special commission on employment. This latter
initiative however was condemned by the whole opposition, including Fabre's own party colleagues, as a manoeuvre by the President

to lure Left-Radicals, discontented with their alliance with the
PCF, into the camp of the *majorité*. The Presidentially-inspired
attempt to secure chairmanships of important Parliamentary committees for the opposition, roles that would greatly have increased
opposition access to information and opposition ability to influence the legislative process, failed.

One day French democracy, if it is to remain democratic,
must solve the problems of 'reasonable cohabitation' and the
peaceful alternation of power. Though he has as yet accomplished
little on terms of action, the President, in his book Démocratie
française[2] and in the conciliatory style of his speeches, has
showed both that he understands the nature of the problem and that
he is determined, if the electors show that it is what they really
want, to prepare his country for peaceful political change.

France has put most of its social divisions behind it.
Conflict over religion or the Republic are footnotes in history.
The people who vote Communist, and indeed the leaders of the
Communist party, show no inclination for revolution as a form of
political action. The country has a stable and effective system
of government and its political institutions are based, for the
first time in modern French history, on wide popular consensus.
There is no need for conflict over a simple matter like a change
of government and there is no need to allow chaos and upheaval to
be its consequence.

NOTES

(1) In two apparent exceptions to this rule there were new candi-
     dates at the by-election (see J-L Parodi 'Les élections par-
     tielles de l'été 1978: surprises et confirmations', Revue
     Politique et Parlementaire, November 1978).

(2) Paris, Fayard, 1976.

APPENDIX

CONSTITUENCY GUIDE

CONSTITUENCY GUIDE

Key -

Normal abbreviations except U = Gaullism 1967-73 (UDVe, UDR), S = Socialists (SFIO CIR, PS)

1978 winner underlined = seat gained

* = Margin of victory less than 5%, ** = less than 1%

++ = 1st ballot victory 1978, + = no *maj.*/opposition second ballot

Départements A. PARIS REGION B. PROVINCES (alphabetical order) C. OVERSEAS FRANCE	Winner in				1978 2nd ball.	Left %			1978 *députés* include:-
	1967	1968	1973	1978	1973	1st ball. 1973	2nd ball. (Pres) 1974	1st ball. 1978	
A. PARIS REGION									
Paris City:						41	43	39	
1 1st & 4th *Arr'ts*	U	U	U	RPR	S	40	43	37	
2 2nd & 3rd	RI	RI	RI	UDF	PC	43	48	36	Dominati
3 5th (Latin Quarter)	U	U	U	RPR	++	39	44	33	
4 6th *Arrondissement*	U	U	U	RPR	+	31	34	28	
5 7th	CD	U	RI	UDF	++	23	27	21	
6 8th	U	U	U	RPR	+	20	25	19	Couve de Murville
7 9th	U	U	U	RPR	S	33	38	31	
8 10th	U	U	U	RPR	S	44	47	42	
9 11th (St Ambroise)	U	U	U	RPR*	S	44	51	47	
10 11th (Ste Marguerite)	PC	U	PC	RPR	PC	50	52	48	
11 12th (Bel-Air)	U	U	U	UDF	S	40	43	39	
12 12th (Bercy)	U	U	U	UDF	S	44	48	44	
13 13th (Salpétrière)	PC	U	PC	PC	RPR	53	57	53	
14 13th (Croulebarbe)	PC	U	U	S*	RPR	49	52	50	
15 14th (Montparnasse)	U	U	CDP	RPR	S	39	42	36	
16 14th (Plaisance)	U	U	U	RPR**	S	49	52	46	
17 15th (St Lambert)	U	U	U	RPR	S	39	42	35	
18 15th (Grenelle)	U	U	U	RPR	S	34	37	29	
19 15th (Javel)	U	U	U	RPR	S	41	43	37	
20 16th (Auteuil)	U	U	CD	UDF	+	20	24	17	
21 16th (Chaillot)	U	U	U	UDF	+	17	21	14	
22 17th (Monceau)	U	U	U	RPR	+	21	26	21	Druon
23 17th (Batignolles)	U	U	U	RPR	+	27	32	27	
24 17th (Epinettes)	U	U	U	RPR	S	42	48	43	
25 18th (Montmartre)	S	U	RI	UDF	S	46	48	42	Chinaud
26 18th (Clignancourt)	U	U	U	RPR	S	48	47	42	

128

A. PARIS REGION (cont'd)		Winner in				1978 2nd ball.	Left %			1978 *députés* include:-
		1967	1968	1973	1978		1st ball. 1973	2nd ball. (Pres) 1974	1st ball. 1978	
27	18th (la Chapelle)	PC	U	PC	UDF*	PC	52	55	51	
28	19th (la Villette)	U	U	PC	UDF*	PC	50	54	54	
29	19th (P de Flandres)	PC	U	PC	PC*	RPR	51	54	56	Laurent
30	20th (Belleville)	PC	U	PC	UDF*	PC	51	54	52	
31	20th (Père Lachaise)	PC	U	PC	PC**	RPR	51	54	51	
	Hauts de Seine:						49	50	48	
1	Gennevilliers	PC	PC	PC	PC	RPR	70	70	73	
2	Asnières	U	U	U	RPR	S	43	46	46	
3	Colombes	U	U	PC	PC**	RPR	54	51	54	
4	Clichy	PC	U	PC	PC**	UDF	55	53	58	
5	Courbevoie	RI	RI	RI	UDF	S	43	44	40	
6	Neuilly	U	U	U	*Maj.*	+	32	44	24	
7	Nanterre	PC	PC	PC	PC	RPR	62	59	61	
8	St Cloud	U	U	U	RPR	S	39	43	38	
9	Sèvres	U	U	U	RPR	S	44	45	39	Labbé
10	Boulogne-Billancourt	U	U	U	RPR	S	40	43	35	
11	Issy, Malakoff	PC	PC	PC	PC*	UDF	55	57	54	
12	Sceaux, Clamart	PC	U	U	UDF*	PC	50	52	48	
13	Antony, Montrouge	U	U	CD	UDF	PC	50	53	49	
	Seine St Denis:						64	62	65	
1	St Ouen, Epinay	PC	PC	PC	PC	RPR	66	64	67	
2	St Denis	PC	PC	PC	PC	+	71	69	71	
3	Aubervilliers	PC	PC	PC	PC	++	72	68	72	
4	Le Bourget	PC	PC	PC	PC	++	73	71	71	
5	Noisy-le-Sec	PC	U	PC	PC	RPR	55	56	62	
6	Bagnolet, Pantin	PC	PC	PC	PC	RPR	61	61	62	
7	Montreuil	PC	PC	PC	PC	UDF	61	60	65	
8	Aulnay-sous-bois	PC	PC	PC	PC	RPR	61	60	63	Ballanger
9	Le Raincy	U	U	U	PC**	RPR	54	54	53	Goutmann
	Val de Marne:						52	55	54	
1	Villejuif	PC	PC	PC	PC	+	61	64	64	Marchais
2	Orly	PC	PC	PC	PC	RPR	59	59	63	Fiterman
3	Ivry	PC	PC	PC	PC	RPR	70	70	72	

A. PARIS REGION (cont'd)	Winner in				1978 2nd ball.	Left %			1978 _députés_ include:-
	1967	1968	1973	1978		1st ball. 1973	2nd ball. (Pres) 1974	1st ball. 1978	
4 Charenton	RI	RI	S	S*	UDF	51	53	52	
5 Créteil	U	U	U	UDF	S	42	48	44	
6 Nogent	U	U	U	RPR	PC	45	51	45	Nungesser
7 Vincennes	U	U	U	RPR	PC	41	42	39	
8 Boissy St Leger	U	U	PC	PC	UDF**	50	55	53	
Seine-et-Marne:						42	49	49	
1 Melun	U	U	S	S*	RPR	44	50	51	
2 Chelles, Lagny	U	U	PC	PC	RPR	51	55	60	
3 Meaux	U	U	U	UDF	S	44	48	49	
4 Provins	U	U	U	RPR	++	32	49	45	Peyrefitte
5 Fontainebleau	U	U	U	RPR	S	38	44	40	
Yvelines:						46	47	43	
1 Maisons-Laffitte	U	U	RI	UDF	PC	48	50	47	
2 St Germain-en-Laye	U	U	U	RPR	S	39	40	35	
3 Poissy	S	U	U	S	RPR	49	52	50	Rocard
4 Marly-le-Roi	U	U	U	RPR	S	42	41	34	
5 Versailles NW	RI	RI	RI	RPR	PC	40	44	38	
6 Versailles SE	U	U	U	RPR	S	39	53	39	
7 Mantes	PC	U	U	RPR*	PC	48	50	49	
8 Rambouillet	Rad	Rad	MRG	UDF*	MRG	66	54	52	
Essonne:						52	54	53	
1 Corbeil	PC	U	PC	PC*	UDF	50	54	54	
2 Arpajon	U	U	U	RPR*	PC	50	51	48	
3 Longjumeau	PC	U	PC	PC	RPR	53	55	57	Juquin
4 Palaiseau	PC	U	PC	PC	UDF	53	54	53	
Val d'Oise:						52	54	52	
1 Pontoise	RI	RI	RI	S*	UDF	45	50	47	
2 Cormeilles	U	U	PC	RPR*	PC	49	52	49	
3 Argenteuil	PC	PC	PC	PC	RPR	68	66	65	
4 Enghien	U	U	U	UDF	S	41	47	41	
5 Sarcelles	PC	U	PC	PC	RPR	55	57	57	

	Winner in				1978 2nd ball.	Left %			1978 *députés* include:-
	1967	1968	1973	1978		1st ball. 1973	2nd ball. (Pres) 1974	1st ball. 1978	

B. PROVINCES (Alphabetical order by Départements)

	Winner in				1978 2nd ball.	1st ball. 1973	2nd ball. (Pres) 1974	1st ball. 1978	1978 *députés* include:-
Ain:						38	45	44	
1 Bourg-en-Bresse	CD	PDM	CDP	RPR*	S	34	45	47	
2 Nantua	RI	RI	RI	UDF	PC	41	45	42	
3 Ambérieux	RI	RI	RI	UDF	MRG	40	45	44	
Aisne:						52	56	57	
1 Laon	U	U	U	S	RPR	47	55	59	
2 St Quentin	U	U	PC	PC	RPR	52	57	55	
3 Vervins	S	S	S	S	UDF	61	55	62	
4 La Fère	U	U	PC	PC	RPR	54	58	57	
5 Soissons	CD	PDM	CD	UDF*	PC	44	54	52	
Allier:						49	54	54	
1 Moulins	PC	U	U	RPR*	PC	51	54	52	Rolland
2 Montluçon	S	PC	Ind	PC	*Maj.*	53	59	59	
3 Gannat	PC	PC	PC	PC*	UDF	58	56	56	
4 Vichy	Rad	Rad	Rad	UDF	PC	34	49	49	Péronnet
Alpes-de-Hte-Provence:						59	54	52	
1 Digne	Rad	Rad	MRG	MRG*	RPR	57	52	50	
2 Manosque	S	S	S	PC*	*Maj.*	60	55	54	
Hautes-Alpes:						43	48	48	
1 Gap	Rad	Rad	CDP	UDF	MRG	47	51	50	
2 Briançon	U	RI	RI	UDF	PC	38	45	45	
Alpes-Maritimes:						38	46	44	
1 Nice 1, 2, 3	PC	PC	PC	UDF	PC	46	51	47	
2 Nice 4, 5	CD	PDM	CD	UDF	S	32	43	39	Médecin
3 Nice 6	S	RI	RI	UDF	PC	45	48	44	
4 Menton	CD	U	U	RPR	PC	43	47	45	
5 Cannes	CD	RI	Ind	UDF	S/Ind	25	44	45	
6 Grasse	U	U	U	RPR	PC	38	46	44	

B. PROVINCES (cont'd)	Winner in 1967	1968	1973	1978	1978 2nd ball.	Left % 1st ball. 1973	2nd ball. (Pres) 1974	1st ball. 1978	1978 *députés* include:-
Ardèche:						42	48	45	
1 Privas	U	U	U	UDF*	PC	50	51	47	
2 Tournon	CD	U	U	UDF	++	38	44	42	
3 Aubenas	CD	U	U	RPR	PC	37	47	46	
Ardennes:						51	54	55	
1 Mézières	U	U	U	<u>PC</u>*	RPR	45	52	55	
2 Charleville	S	S	S	<u>PC</u>	RPR	59	57	60	
3 Sedan	PSU	U	U	RPR*	S	48	51	51	
Ariège:						66	64	67	
1 Foix	S	S	S	S	RPR	67	65	64	
2 Pamiers	S	S	S	S	RPR	64	63	70	
Aube:						47	49	46	
1 Troyes 1	U	U	S	<u>UDF</u>*	S	44	48	48	
2 Troyes 3	S	U	U	RPR	++	46	49	45	Galley
3 Troyes 2, Nogent	U	U	U	UDF	PC	51	50	46	
Aude:						62	62	64	
1 Carcassonne	S	S	S	S	RPR	66	62	64	
2 Narbonne	S	S	S	S	+	66	65	69	
3 Castelnaudary	S	U	S	S	RPR	53	58	59	
Aveyron:						36	43	50	
1 Rodez	RI	RI	CD	UDF	S	22	36	34	
2 Villefranche	Rad	Rad	MRG	MRG	UDF	55	53	66	Fabre
3 Millau	U	U	U	RPR	S	32	42	50	
Bouches-du-Rhône:						60	56	58	
1 Marseille 1, 6	S	U	U	RPR	S	41	43	41	
2 Marseille 8, 9, 6	S	U	S	<u>UDF</u>	S	48	47	46	
3 Marseille 2, 7	S	S	S	S	RPR	62	56	58	Defferre
4 Marseille 14, 15, 16	PC	PC	PC	PC	++	74	71	76	

132

B. PROVINCES (cont'd)	Winner in				1978 2nd ball.	Left % 1st ball. 1973	2nd ball. (Pres) 1974	1st ball. 1978	1978 *députés* include:-
	1967	1968	1973	1978					
5 Marseille 5, 10	PC	RI	PC	PC	UDF	59	57	56	
6 Marseille 11	PC	PC	PC	PC	UDF	66	58	64	
7 Marseille 3, 4	PC	PC	PC	PC	RPR	66	62	64	
8 Marseille 12, 13, 14	S	S	S	PC	UDF	61	56	58	
9 Aix-en-Provence	S	S	S	S*	UDF	59	52	52	
10 Salon, Martigues	PC	PC	PC	PC	RPR	64	60	65	
11 Arles	S	S	PC	PC	UDF	65	57	59	
Calvados:						38	44	40	
1 Caen	U	U	S	S*	RPR	46	49	47	
2 Lisieux	U	U	U	RPR*	S	42	47	47	
3 Trouville	RI	RI	RI	UDF	S	40	45	46	d'Ornano
4 Bayeux	U	U	Ind	UDF	++	25	39	33	
5 Vire	CD	U	U	UDF	++	21	37	27	Stirn
Cantal:						34	38	40	
1 Aurillac	U	U	U	RPR	++	34	42	45	
2 St Flour	U	U	U	RPR	++	34	35	35	
Charente:						42	54	53	
1 Angoulême	U	U	U	S	RPR	43	53	52	
2 Cognac	Rad	Rad	U	RPR	PC	38	51	52	
3 Confolens	U	U	U	PC	RPR	46	57	55	
Charente-Maritime:						40	50	50	
1 La Rochelle	U	U	MRG	MRG	RPR	59	51	59	Crêpeau
2 Rochefort	U	U	U	RPR	S	39	50	45	
3 St Jean d'Angely	CD	PDM	CDP	S*	RPR	35	52	52	
4 Saintes	S	RI	RI	S*	UDF	38	51	51	
5 Royan	U	U	U	RPR	PC	29	45	43	
Cher:						46	51	53	
1 Bourges	RI	RI	RI	UDF*	PC	44	51	53	
2 Vierzon	U	U	U	RPR*	PC	46	52	53	
3 St Amand	PC	U	U	RPR*	PC	48	53	52	

B. PROVINCES (cont'd)	Winner in				1978 2nd ball.	Left %			1978 *députés* include:-
	1967	1968	1973	1978		1st ball. 1973	2nd ball. (Pres) 1974	1st ball. 1978	
Corrèze:						47	56	55	
1 Tulle	S	S	PC	RPR**	PC	47	58	55	
2 Brive	S	U	U	PC*	RPR	46	55	67	
3 Ussel	U	U	U	RPR	++	47	47	43	Chirac
Corse du Sud:New *Département*									
1 Ajaccio	U	U	MRG	RPR*	MRG	36	46	41	
2 Sartène	U	U	U	RPR	++	37	41	40	
Haute-Corse: New *Département*									
1 Bastia	Rad	U	MRG	RPR*	MRG	51	47	46	
2 Corte (new seat)				RPR*	MRG	40	47	51	
Côte d'Or:						42	48	46	
1 Dijon SW	U	U	U	RPR	S	43	49	43	Poujade
2 Dijon NE	U	U	U	RPR	S	44	48	48	
3 Beaune	Rad	U	U	*Maj.*	MRG	41	47	46	Lecat
4 Montbard	Rad	RI	RI	UDF	PC	40	49	48	
Côtes du Nord:						49	50	52	
1 St Brieuc	PSU	U	PSU	UDF	PC	54	48	54	
2 Dinan	CD	CD	S	UDF*	S	46	47	51	
3 Loudéac	U	U	U	RPR*	S	43	48	47	
4 Guingamp	CD	PDM	CDP	PC*	UDF	51	56	54	
5 Lannion	CD	PDM	CDP	S*	UDF	49	52	53	
Creuse:						61	56	59	
1 Guéret	U	U	S	RPR**	S	52	54	54	
2 Aubusson	S	S	S	S	RPR	70	58	64	Chandernagor
Dordogne:						52	56	58	
1 Périgueux	U	U	U	RPR**	PCF	48	55	53	Guéna
2 Bergerac	S	U	S	S	RPR	48	54	59	
3 Nontron	Rad	U	MRG	MRG	RPR	58	55	62	
4 Sarlat	S	U	PC	PC	RPR	53	58	59	

134

B. PROVINCES (cont'd)	Winner in				1978 2nd ball.	1st ball. 1973	2nd ball. (Pres) 1974	1st ball. 1978	1978 *députés* include:-
	1967	1968	1973	1978					
Doubs:						46	48	49	
1 Besançon	U	U	U	RPR*	S	44	45	49	
2 Montbéliard	S	S	S	S	RPR	66	58	61	
3 Pontarlier	U	U	U	RPR	++	28	34	38	E. Faure
Drôme:						50	52	53	
1 Valence	U	U	U	S	RPR	50	51	49	
2 Montélimar	S	S	S	S	RPR	52	53	52	
3 Romans-sur-Isère	S	U	S	S	UDF	48	51	57	
Eure:						41	49	48	
1 Evreux	RI	RI	RI	UDF	PC	45	52	48	
2 Bernay	R	R	S	S**	UDF	38	52	51	
3 Louviers	CD	U	CD	UDF**	MRG	43	52	47	
4 Les Andelys	U	U	U	RPR	PC	38	48	46	
Eure-et-Loir:						38	48	48	
1 Chartres	Rad	RI	RI	S*	UDF	38	48	48	
2 Dreux	S	U	S	RPR*	S	43	48	48	
3 Châteaudun	U	U	U	UDF	MRG	34	48	47	
Finistère:						40	42	44	
1 Quimper	U	U	U	RPR	++	43	47	45	Bécam
2 Brest	CD	U	U	UDF**	S	45	46	50	
3 Landernau	U	U	U	RPR	S	16	26	32	
4 Morlaix	PSU	U	U	S**	UDF	52	50	50	
5 Landivisiau	U	U	U	RPR	S	28	28	27	
6 Châteaulin	U	U	U	RPR	PC	42	45	45	
7 Douarnenez	U	U	U	RPR	PC	42	40	39	
8 Quimperlé	CD	RI	S	S	UDF	54	51	62	
Gard:						59	56	59	
1 Nîmes	S	U	PC	PC**	RPR	58	52	53	
2 Bagnols	CD	PDM	S	PC*	UDF	52	56	54	
3 Alès E	PC	PC	PC	PC	UDF	65	59	66	

B. PROVINCES (cont'd)	Winner in				1978 2nd ball.	Left %			1978 *députés* include:-
	1967	1968	1973	1978		1st ball. 1973	2nd ball. (Pres) 1974	1st ball. 1978	
4 Alès W	PC	U	PC	PC	RPR	60	57	63	
Haute-Garonne:						52	56	54	
1 Toulouse N	S	U	S	S*	UDF	51	52	50	Savary
2 Toulouse Central	S	RI	RI	S*	UDF	46	54	49	
3 Toulouse S	S	U	S	S*	RPR	47	52	50	
4 Toulouse W	S	S	S	S	RPR	62	61	54	
5 Muret	Ind	Ind	S	S	Maj	49	59	56	
6 St Gaudens	Rad	Rad	S	S	RPR	59	60	62	
Gers:						47	58	53	
1 Auch	S	S	S	S	RPR	50	57	58	
2 Condom	CD	PDM	CDP	S*	*Maj.*	44	53	48	
Gironde:						47	55	51	
1 Bordeaux 1, 2	U	U	U	RPR	S	42	47	43	
2 Bordeaux 3, 4	U	U	U	RPR	++	34	45	34	Chaban-Delmas
3 Bordeaux 5, 6	S	U	S	S	RPR	52	54	52	
4 Bordeaux 7	S	S	S	S	RPR	68	65	66	
5 Médoc	CD	PDM	CDP	MRG**	UDF	41	53	43	
6 Mérignac	S	S	S	S	RPR	55	60	62	
7 Arcachon	CD	PDM	RI	RPR*	S	40	50	46	
8 Langon	S	S	S	S	UDF	56	58	63	
9 Libourne	U	U	U	RPR**	S	44	53	51	Boulin
10 Blaye	S	U	U	S	UDF	40	55	52	
Hérault:						58	55	58	
1 Montpellier, Lunel	Rad	U	S	UDF**	S	46	49	50	
2 Montpellier, Lodève	S	U	S	S	UDF	55	52	57	
3 Sète	PC	U	PC	PC	UDF	61	58	60	
4 Béziers 1	PC	U	PC	PC	UDF	56	56	56	
5 Béziers 2	S	S	S	S	UDF	74	62	69	
Ille-et-Vilaine:						29	38	37	
1 Rennes N	CD	U	U	RPR	S	38	44	47	

B. PROVINCES (cont'd)	Winner in				1978 in 2nd ball.	Left % 1st ball. 1973	2nd ball. (Pres) 1974	1st ball. 1978	1978 députés include:-
	1967	1968	1973	1978					
2 Rennes S	U	U	U	RPR	S	39	45	47	
3 Vitré	CD	U	CDP	UDF	++	19	22	24	Méhaignerie
4 Redon	RI	RI	RI	UDF	S	22	31	29	
5 Fougères	U	U	U	RPR	S	22	32	34	
6 St Malô	U	U	U	RPR	++	33	42	40	Bourges
Indre:						48	52	52	
1 Chateauroux	U	U	PC	RPR*	PC	51	51	50	
2 Issoudun	PC	RI	RI	UDF*	PC	51	53	54	
3 Le Blanc	Ind	U	U	RPR*	S	42	52	51	
Indre-et-Loire:						43	47	47	
1 Tours	Maj.	Maj.	Maj.	Maj.	S	40	47	43	Royer
2 Langeais	U	U	U	UDF*	S	43	46	49	
3 Amboise	Rad	Rad	MRG	RPR*	S	50	49	48	
4 Chinon	U	U	U	RPR	S	38	46	46	
Isère:						51	53	52	
1 Grenoble E	RI	RI	RI	UDF**	S	48	50	47	
2 Grenoble S	PSU	U	S	S	RPR	57	52	56	Dubedout
3 La Mure	PC	U	PC	PC	RPR	56	55	58	
4 Grenoble N	S	U	S	S	RPR	47	48	53	
5 Vienne N	S	U	S	S	UDF	57	53	54	Mermaz
6 Vienne S	PC	RI	RI	S*	UDF	51	53	53	
7 La Tour du Pin	RI	RI	RI	UDF	S	41	49	45	
Jura:						40	49	49	
1 Lons-le-Saunier	RI	RI	RI	UDF	S	43	48	46	
2 Dôle	CD	PDM	CDP	UDF*	S	37	50	51	
Landes:						42	53	56	
1 Mont de Marsan	S	U	U	S*	RPR	34	52	52	
2 Dax	S	S	S	S	UDF	61	53	61	
3 Aire-sur-l'Adour	CD	PDM	CDP	S**	UDF	30	54	54	

137

B. PROVINCES (cont'd)	Winner in				1978 2nd ball.	Left %			1978 *députés* include:-
	1967	1968	1973	1978		1st ball. 1973	2nd ball. (Pres) 1974	1st ball. 1978	
Loir-et-Cher:						44	49	48	
1 Blois	CD	PDM	CDP	UDF	++	41	49	48	Sudreau
2 Romorantin	S	U	U	RPR	++	45	50	50	
3 Vendôme	S	CD	CDP	UDF	S	45	47	47	
Loire:						43	48	47	
1 St Etienne N	Ind	PDM	Rad	UDF	PC	41	51	46	Durafour
2 St Etienne S	U	U	U	RPR	PC	45	49	51	
3 St Chamond	CD	PDM	CDP	UDF	S	43	48	44	
4 Firminy	CD	PDM	CDP	<u>PC</u>	UDF	56	53	57	
5 Roanne	U	U	U	<u>S**</u>	RPR	41	49	49	
6 Feurs	U	U	U	<u>UDF</u>	S	36	43	41	
7 Montbrison	CD	CD	RI	UDF	MRG	36	42	39	
Haute-Loire:						38	40	42	
1 Le Puy SE	CD	CD	CDP	UDF	++	28	38	35	Barrot
2 Le Puy NW	S	S	RI	UDF	++	48	43	48	
Loire-Atlantique:						36	43	44	
1 Nantes Central	U	U	U	RPR	S	43	48	45	
2 Nantes W	S	U	S	S*	RPR	48	51	49	
3 Nantes S	U	U	U	<u>S**</u>	RPR	46	51	53	
4 Ancenis	RI	RI	RI	UDF	S	24	32	38	
5 Châteaubriant	U	U	U	*Maj.*	++	27	36	35	
6 St Nazaire	S	S	S	S	RPR	54	56	56	
7 La Baule	U	U	U	RPR	++	27	37	41	Guichard
8 Pornic	U	U	U	RPR	S	21	30	29	
Loiret:						43	45	45	
1 Orléans E	U	U	U	<u>UDF</u>	S	45	43	46	
2 Orléans W	U	U	U	RPR	PC	49	46	50	
3 Pithiviers	U	U	U	RPR	S	35	42	40	
4 Montargis	U	U	U	RPR	PC	44	47	44	

B. PROVINCES (cont'd)	Winner in				1978 2nd ball.	Left %			1978 députés include:-
	1967	1968	1973	1978		1st ball. 1973	2nd ball. (Pres) 1974	1st ball. 1978	
Lot:						56	54	59	
1 Cahors	Rad	Rad	MRG	MRG	RPR	60	55	60	M. Faure
2 Figeac	U	U	U	S	RPR	51	53	57	
Lot-et-Garonne:						47	55	52	
1 Agen	Rad	U	S	S	RPR	48	54	53	
2 Marmande	PC	U	PC	PC	RPR	50	57	58	
3 Villeneuve-sur-Lot	Rad	Rad	Rad	S*	RPR	44	54	46	
Lozère:						23	36	37	
1 Mende	RI	RI	RI	UDF	++	30	40	40	
2 Marjevols	U	U	RI	UDF	++	15	30	33	Blanc
Maine-et-Loire:						27	37	38	
1 Angers NE	U	U	U	RPR	S	38	42	44	
2 Angers S	U	U	U	RPR	++	32	36	40	
3 Saumur N	U	U	U	UDF	S	29	43	38	
4 Saumur S	U	U	CD	UDF	++	11	34	31	
5 Cholet	U	U	Ind	Maj.	++	19	30	32	
6 Angers W	U	U	U	RPR	++	33	38	42	
Manche:						29	35	32	
1 St Lô	U	U	CD	UDF	S	27	31	34	
2 Avranches	U	U	U	RPR	+	17	28	21	
3 Coutances	U	U	RI	UDF	S	24	34	32	
4 Valognes	U	U	U	RPR	S	28	32	28	
5 Cherbourg	U	U	S	S**	UDF	49	49	47	
Marne:						46	49	47	
1 Reims 1, 3	U	U	U	UDF	PC	44	50	49	
2 Reims 2, 4	U	U	U	RPR	PC	45	50	45	
3 Châlons-sur-Marne	U	U	U	RPR	PC	47	48	47	
4 Epernay	PC	U	CDP	UDF	PC	46	48	45	
Haute-Marne:						42	48	48	
1 Chaumont	U	U	U	UDF	S	35	46	44	

139

B. PROVINCES (cont'd)	Winner in				1978 2nd ball.	Left % 1st ball. 1973	2nd ball. (Pres) 1974	1st ball. 1978	1978 *députés* include:-
	1967	1968	1973	1978					
2　St Dizier	U	U	U	RPR	PC	48	50	52	
Mayenne:						28	33	38	
1　Laval	U	U	U	UDF	S	45	38	45	
2　Château-Gontier	U	U	U	RPR	++	16	27	31	
3　Mayenne	RI	RI	RI	UDF	++	22	32	37	
Meurthe-et-Moselle:						43	51	52	
1　Nancy N	U	U	Rad	UDF**	S	37	49	50	Servan-Schreiber (- beaten in re-run Sept. 1978)
2　Nancy W	U	U	RI	UDF*	S	44	48	53	
3　Nancy SE	RI	RI	RI	UDF	S	35	45	46	
4　Lunéville	RI	RI	RI	UDF	++	37	44	46	Haby
5　Toul	RI	U	U	UDF	S	35	44	40	Bigeard
6　Briey	PC	RI	PC	PC	UDF	59	64	68	
7　Longwy	U	U	Rad	PC	UDF	54	61	64	
Meuse:						42	46	48	
1　Bar-le-Duc	U	U	S	UDF*	S	42	46	48	
2　Verdun	RI	RI	RI	UDF	S	41	46	47	
Morbihan:						32	38	38	
1　Vannes	RI	RI	RI	UDF	S	23	28	36	
2　Auray	RI	RI	RI	UDF	++	28	36	30	Bonnet
3　Pontivy	U	U	U	RPR	S	30	35	35	
4　Ploermel	RI	RI	CD	UDF	S	13	28	22	
5　Lorient	S	RI	S	S	RPR	57	48	55	
6　Hennebont	CD	CD	CD	UDF	PC	43	51	51	
Moselle:						32	46	42	
1　Metz 1, 2	RI	RI	CD	S*	UDF	36	50	51	
2　Metz 3	CD	U	U	RPR	S	29	41	35	
3　Thionville W	PC	RI	PC	PC	UDF	59	61	65	
4　Thionville E	RI	RI	RI	UDF	PC	42	49	46	
5　St Avold	U	U	U	RPR	S	33	49	43	
6　Forbach	U	U	CD	RPR	S	29	47	38	

B. PROVINCES (cont'd)	Winner in				1978 2nd ball.	Left %			1978 *députés* include:-
						1st ball. 1973	2nd ball. (Pres) 1974	1st ball. 1978	
	1967	1968	1973	1978					
7 Sarreguemines	U	U	CDP	UDF	S	15	38	30	
8 Sarrebourg	Ind	U	U	RPR	++	13	27	26	Messmer
Nièvre:						61	61	62	
1 Nevers	S	S	S	S	UDF	64	61	63	
2 Cosne	PC	U	S	S	UDF	57	60	62	
3 Château-Chinon	S	S	S	S	*Maj.*	61	64	62	Mitterrand
Nord:						52	54	56	
1 Lille Central	U	U	U	RPR	++	38	40	38	Segard
2 Lille S	U	U	S	S	RPR	52	52	58	Mauroy
3 Lille N	U	U	U	RPR	S	42	46	48	
4 Lille E	S	U	S	S	RPR	54	54	63	
5 Hambourdin	S	S	S	S	UDF	61	57	62	
6 Seclin	S	U	S	S	RPR	52	53	56	
7 Roubaix E	U	U	S	S*	UDF	50	52	52	
8 Roubaix NW	S	U	S	S*	UDF	51	53	55	
9 Tourcoing	U	U	U	RPR	S	37	43	41	
10 Armentières	U	U	S	S**	RPR	47	50	52	
11 Dunkerque	S	S	S	S	*Maj.*	57	56	57	
12 Bourbourg	U	U	U	RPR	S	38	40	44	
13 Hazebrouck	U	U	U	*Maj.*	S	39	44	46	
14 Douai NW	PC	PC	PC	PC	RPR	56	60	58	
15 Douai S	PC	PC	PC	PC	RPR	63	64	66	
16 Cambrai	S	S	U	RPR**	PC	62	56	55	
17 Le Cateau	PC	RI	RI	PC*	UDF	54	57	60	
18 Valenciennes	PC	PC	PC	PC	RPR	58	59	59	
19 St Amand	PC	PC	CD	PC	UDF	50	60	55	
20 Denain	PC	PC	PC	PC	RPR	70	67	71	Ansart
21 Avesnes	S	U	S	PC*	RPR	53	56	61	
22 Maubeuge	S	U	PC	PC	RPR	57	58	59	
23 Le Quesnoy	PC	U	PC	PC	UDF	56	59	66	
Oise:						45	53	49	
1 Beauvais NE	U	U	U	RPR	++	40	51	43	Dassault
2 Compiègne	U	U	U	S*	UDF	41	50	50	

B. PROVINCES (cont'd)	Winner in				1978 2nd ball.	Left % 1st ball. 1973	2nd ball. (Pres) 1974	1st ball. 1978	1978 *députés* include:-
	1967	1968	1973	1978					
3 Clermont	Rad	CD	CDP	PC	UDF	49	56	50	
4 Senlis	U	U	U	RPR**	PC	52	53	55	
5 Beauvais SW	U	U	U	RPR*	PC	43	52	46	
Orne:						28	39	37	
1 Alençon	U	U	U	RPR	S	26	37	39	
2 Mortagne	CD	CD	CD	UDF	S	26	41	36	
3 Flers	CD	CD	U	UDF	S	33	37	37	
Pas-de-Calais:						61	58	65	
1 Arras	S	S	S	S	UDF	61	56	58	
2 Bapaume	S	U	U	MRG*	RPR	44	52	53	
3 St Pol	PC	RI	S	S	RPR	56	54	61	
4 Le Touquet	U	U	U	S**	UDF	40	48	47	
5 Boulogne S	S	S	PC	PC	RPR	62	57	62	
6 Boulogne N	S	U	S	S	RPR	52	53	58	
7 Calais	U	U	PC	PC	UDF	53	53	61	
8 St Omer	S	U	S	S	RPR	53	55	63	
9 Béthune	PC	U	PC	S	UDF	57	57	67	
10 Bruay-en-Artois	PC	PC	PC	PC	+	78	65	77	
11 Cambrai	PC	PC	PC	PC	UDF	66	64	70	
12 Liévin	S	S	S	S	+	81	72	77	
13 Lens	S	S	S	S	RPR	81	66	78	
14 Henin-Liétard	S	S	PC	PC	RPR	71	64	77	
Puy-de-Dôme:						54	48	53	
1 Clermont E & S	S	S	S	S	RPR	61	52	61	
2 Clermont N & SW	RI	RI	RI	UDF	++	40	39	41	
3 Issoire	Rad	S	S	S	UDF	58	50	57	
4 Thiers	S	S	S	UDF*	S	57	48	52	
5 Riom	RI	RI	S	S	UDF	52	49	55	
Pyrenées-Atlantiques:						35	44	43	
1 Pau	S	PDM	S	S**	RPR	50	47	49	
2 Oloron	Rad	U	U	RPR*	S	33	49	48	
3 Mauléon	U	U	U	RPR	S	20	31	31	

B. PROVINCES (cont'd)	Winner in				1978 2nd ball.	Left %			1978 *députés* include:-
	1967	1968	1973	1978		1st ball. 1973	2nd ball. (Pres) 1974	1st ball. 1978	
4 Bayonne	U	U	U	RPR	S	35	42	44	
Hautes-Pyrénées:						54	57	59	
1 Tarbes	Rad	Rad	S	S	UDF	51	58	56	
2 Lourdes	S	U	MRG	MRG	RPR	56	56	61	
Pyrénées-Orientales:						61	57	54	
1 Perpignan E	CD	S	S	Ind	PC	64	56	49	Alduy
2 Perpignan W	PC	U	PC	PC	UDF	57	57	59	
Bas-Rhin:						21	33	27	
1 Strasbourg N & S	U	U	U	UDF	S	27	33	30	
2 Strasbourg E & W	U	U	U	RPR	S	33	41	36	Bord
3 Strasbourg rural	U	U	U	RPR	S	29	39	34	
4 Sélestat	U	U	U	UDF	S	18	28	29	
5 Molsheim	U	U	CD	UDF	S	17	29	25	
6 Saverne	U	U	CD	*Maj.*	++	15	33	18	
7 Wissembourg	U	U	U	RPR	++	13	26	21	
8 Haguenau	U	U	U	RPR	++	18	29	24	
Haut-Rhin:						21	34	31	
1 Colmar	U	U	CD	UDF	S	19	30	29	
2 Guebwiller	U	U	U	UDF	S	26	37	32	
3 Altkirch	U	U	U	RPR	S	19	31	30	
4 Mulhouse	U	U	Ind	UDF	S	14	38	33	
5 Mulhouse rural	U	U	U	RPR	S	28	36	33	
Rhône:						45	47	45	
1 Lyon 1, 12, 13	U	U	U	RPR*	PC	47	50	48	
2 Lyon 2, 5, 6	U	U	U	UDF	S	42	48	44	
3 Lyon 3, 4	U	U	Ind	RPR	S	38	43	36	
4 Lyon 7, 8, 11	U	U	U	UDF	++	33	37	32	Barre
5 Lyon 9, 10	U	U	U	RPR	++	39	41	38	
6 Villeurbanne	PC	PC	CD	S	UDF	51	54	56	Hernu
7 Limonest	U	U	Rad	UDF	S	37	42	41	
8 Givors	RI	RI	RI	UDF	++	37	43	40	
9 Tarare	Rad	U	RI	UDF	++	46	41	35	

B. PROVINCES (cont'd)	Winner in				1978 2nd ball.	Left %			1978 *députés* include:-
	1967	1968	1973	1978		1st ball. 1973	2nd ball. (Pres) 1974	1st ball. 1978	
10 Villefranche/Saône	Rad	RI	RI	UDF	S	40	45	46	
11 Vénissieux	(new seat 1973)		PC	PC	RPR	70	65	69	
12 Francheville	"	"	"	U	RPR*	S	45	47	46	
13 Bron	"	"	"	S	S	RPR	58	56	60	J. Poperen
Haute-Saône:						45	50	49	
1 Vesoul	RI	RI	RI	UDF*	S	38	47	48	
2 Luxeuil-les-Bains	Rad	U	CDP	UDF*	S	51	53	50	
Saône-et-Loire:						49	51	52	
1 Macon	S	RI	RI	UDF	S	48	48	46	Malaud
2 Charolles	Rad	Rad	MRG	MRG	RPR	65	49	57	
3 Le Creusot	Rad	U	U	S	RPR	39	54	52	
4 Monceau-les-Mines	U	U	U	RPR**	S	49	53	52	
5 Châlon-sur-Saône	S	U	S	S*	RPR	46	51	53	Joxe
Sarthe:						43	49	46	
1 Le Mans 1	U	U	U	RPR	++	39	41	46	
2 Le Mans 3	PC	U	U	PC	RPR	53	56	58	
3 La Flèche	S	PDM	CDP	UDF*	S	48	49	46	
4 Le Mans 2	U	U	U	RPR	++	39	49	45	Le Theule
5 Mamers	RI	RI	RI	RPR	S	34	46	37	
Savoie:						48	49	49	
1 Chambéry N	RI	RI	S	S*	RPR	50	47	49	
2 Albertville	CD	CD	CDP	RPR	S	45	49	49	
3 Chambéry S	U	U	S	S*	RPR	49	52	49	
Haute-Savoie:						38	41	37	
1 Annecy	CD	RI	RI	UDF	++	34	40	34	
2 Thonon-les-Bains	RI	RI	RI	UDF	++	40	40	39	
3 Annemasse	U	U	U	UDF*	S	40	42	39	
Seine-Maritime:						48	53	54	
1 Rouen 2, 4	U	U	CD	UDF	S	35	47	44	

144

B. PROVINCES (cont'd)	Winner in				1978 2nd ball.	Left %			1978 *députés* include:-
	1967	1968	1973	1978		1st ball. 1973	2nd ball. (Pres) 1974	1st ball. 1978	
2 Elbeuf	S	S	S	S	UDF	68	60	66	
3 Rouen 1, 3, 6	PC	PC	PC	PC	UDF	55	58	61	Leroy
4 Maromme	PC	U	CD	PC**	UDF	49	54	56	
5 Fécamp	RI	RI	RI	UDF*	S	40	50	49	
6 Le Havre 1,2,5,6,7	U	U	U	RPR	PC	44	47	48	Rufenacht
7 Le Havre 3,4	PC	PC	PC	PC	++	69	68	74	
8 Yvetot	U	U	U	RPR	S	38	47	44	
9 Dieppe	U	U	U	PC*	RPR	47	52	52	
10 Neufchâtel	U	U	U	RPR	S	39	46	41	
Deux-Sèvres:						42	42	49	
1 Niort	U	U	S	S*	UDF	45	50	53	
2 Parthenay	CD	CD	CDP	UDF	++	40	40	41	
3 Bressuire	U	U	CD	UDF	++	26	34	37	
Somme:						46	54	52	
1 Amiens	PC	PC	PC	PC	UDF	54	54	56	
2 Montdidier	U	U	U	RPR**	PC	48	53	53	
3 Ault	PC	U	U	PC*	RPR	49	56	54	
4 Abbeville	S	S	Ref	PC	RPR	33	54	49	
5 Péronne	U	U	U	*Maj.*	PC	46	54	48	
Tarn:						50	51	54	
1 Albi	S	U	S	S	RPR	51	54	62	
2 Castres	U	U	U	RPR	S	43	47	44	
3 Gaillac	S	S	S	S	UDF	57	52	56	
Tarn-et-Garonne:						48	52	53	
1 Montauban	S	U	U	RPR	S	50	48	49	
2 Castelsarrasin	Rad	Rad	MRG	MRG*	RPR	45	55	56	
Var:						50	51	47	
1 Draguignan	S	S	S	S	UDF	60	56	57	
2 Hyères	S	U	U	UDF	S	44	46	39	
3 Toulon-la Garde	U	U	U	UDF	PC	45	49	41	

145

B. PROVINCES (cont'd)	Winner in				1978 2nd ball.	Left %			1978 *députés* include:-
	1967	1968	1973	1978		1st ball. 1973	2nd ball. (Pres) 1974	1st ball. 1978	
4 Toulon - La Seyne	PC	U	PC	UDF	PC	50	52	50	
Vaucluse:						51	54	52	
1 Avignon	S	U	S	S*	RPR	55	54	57	
2 Carpentras	S	U	S	UDF*	PC	46	53	47	
3 Orange	PC	U	U	PC*	RPR	53	55	53	
Vendée:						25	33	34	
1 La Roche-sur-Yon	RI	RI	RI	UDF	S	28	34	36	
2 Fontenay-le-Comte	U	U	CDP	UDF	++	34	45	41	
3 Sables d'Olonne	U	U	U	RPR	S	24	34	32	
4 North Vendée	U	U	U	RPR	++	15	20	26	
Vienne:						44	48	49	
1 Poitiers	U	U	U	S*	UDF	42	47	52	
2 Châtellerault	CD	PDM	CD	UDF*	S	38	49	46	
3 Montmorillon	U	U	U	RPR*	S	52	49	49	
Haute-Vienne:						64	60	63	
1 Limoges E	S	S	PC	PC	RPR	63	60	68	
2 St Junien	PC	U	PC	PC	RPR	57	60	65	
3 Limoges W	S	S	S	PC	RPR	72	60	62	
Vosges:						40	55	45	
1 Epinal	U	U	U	RPR*	S	47	47	45	
2 St Dié	U	U	U	S*	UDF	53	50	50	
3 Remiremont	U	U	U	RPR	S	29	44	43	
4 Vittel	RI	RI	RI	UDF*	S	30	43	43	
Yonne:						41	47	46	
1 Auxerre	S	RI	RI	UDF	S	39	48	44	Soisson
2 Avallon	RI	RI	RI	UDF*	S	42	48	47	
3 Sens	U	U	U	RPR	PC	41	46	48	

B. PROVINCES (cont'd) C. OVERSEAS FRANCE	Winner in				1978 2nd ball.	Left % 1st ball.	2nd ball. (Pres)	1st ball.	1978 *députés* include:-
	1967	1968	1973	1978		1973	1974	1978	
Territoire-de-Belfort:						52	53	55	
1 Belfort	S	U	S	S	UDF	51	53	55	Chevènement
2 Belfort rural	U	U	S	S	UDF	52	54	54	
C. OVERSEAS DEPARTMENTS AND TERRITORIES									
Guadeloupe:						42	56	38	
1 Pointe-à-Pitre	U	U	PC	<u>RPR</u>	PC	54	56	37	
2 les Abymes	PC	PC	S	RPR*	S	50	70	52	
3 Basse-Terre	U	U	U	RPR	Ind	30	43	29	
Guyane:	U	U	U	RPR	++	44	47	43	
Martinique:						36	43	35	
1 North	U	U	U	RPR	++	25	35	19	
2 Fort-de-France	S	S	S	S	++	50	50	54	Césaire
Réunion:						37	50	40	
1 St Denis	U	U	U	RPR	++	31	47	37	Debrē
2 St Paul	U	U	U	UDF	++	48	56	50	
3 St Pierre	U	U	CDP	UDF	++	30	49	36	
St Pierre-et-Miquelon:	U	U	U	<u>S</u>*	UDF	-	25	54	
Nouvelle-Calèdonie:						11	50	11	
1 East Coast	CD	PDM	CD	Ind	RPR	-	-	-	
2 Nouméa (new seat)				*Maj.*	++			14	
Polynésie-Française:						-	51	7	
1 Papeete	RI	PDM	CD	UDF	++	-	-	8	
2 Tahiti (new seat)				RPR	++			6	
Wallis-et-Futuna:	U	U	U	RPR	++	-	5	-	
Mayotte (new seat):				UDF	++	-	-	-	

BIBLIOGRAPHY

The following is a selection of journals and books which have had
articles or entire issues devoted to the French elections of
March 1978:

Projet, juin 1978 (A. Lancelot, R. Rémond, J. Jaffré)

Pouvoirs, 1978

Revue Politique et Parlementaire, juin 1978 (G. le Gall);
   nov. 1978 (J-L Parodi)

Government and Opposition, Summer 1978 (J.R. Frears)

West European Politics, Oct. 1978 (V. Wright)

Revue Française de Science Politique, déc. 1978

H. Penniman (ed.): France at the Polls, Washington DC, 1978

Cahiers du Communisme, avril 1978

Sondages - Revue Française de l'opinion publique, 1978, No. 1

Sources for election statistics:

le Monde: Les élections legislatives de mars 1978 (Dossiers
   et Documents, mars 1978)

le Matin de Paris: Le dossier des législatives 1978

Cahiers du Communisme: Elections législatives mars 1978

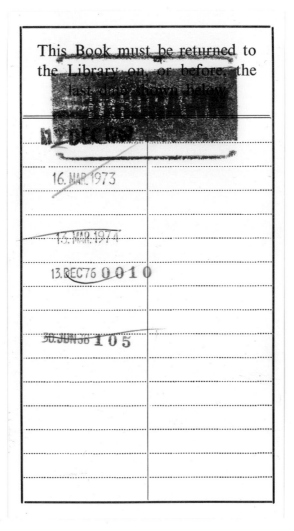